Meditations
on the
Sunday Gospels

Meditations on the Sunday Gospels

Year C

compiled and edited by
John E. Rotelle, O.S.A.

New City Press

Published in the United States by New City Press
202 Cardinal Rd., Hyde Park, NY 12538
©1998 Augustinian Heritage Institute

Cover art: Notre Dame Basillica stained glass, 1885
Cover designed by Nick Cianfarani

Library of Congress Cataloging-in-Publication Data:

Meditations on the Sunday Gospels / introduced and edited by John E.
  Rotelle.

  Includes bibliographical references and index.
  Contents: [1] Year C.
  ISBN 1-56548-086-4 (v. 3 : pbk.)
  1. Church year meditations. 2. Bible. N.T. Gospels
—Meditations. 3. Catholic Church—Prayer-books and devotions
—English.   I. Rotelle, John E.
BX2170.C55M43   1995
242'.3—dc20   95-9013

Printed in Canada

Contents

Feasts which may replace a Sunday

Foreword

From the earliest days of Christianity there has always been an emphasis on reading. The New Testament was written so that people would be able to reflect on it; from century to century it was copied and brought to other parts of the world. The writings of the Greek, Latin, Syriac, and other Church writers were also copied and transported from monastery to monastery, from city to city, from country to country. All this was done so that people would have access to the wisdom and insights of these Church writers.

With an anthology of readings you do much the same thing. You take the best of Church writers over the centuries and present these excellent and timely writings to posterity.

In this present collection of readings I selected those readings which best accompany the gospel passage for each Sunday of the three-year cycle of gospel readings and which convey some kind of message for our day and age. The reading is aligned with each gospel passage which is given in summary form at the very beginning. At times the gospel passage has one theme; where there are several themes in the gospel passage, a choice of one theme or other has to be made. The reading is not a commentary, in the strict sense, on the gospel; the reading was selected as a reflection, meditation, or elongation of the gospel.

I purposely stayed within the framework of what historians call the modern era—seventeenth to the twentieth centuries. At times I did select, by way of exception, some readings from earlier centuries. My reason for staying within this framework is twofold: First, I wanted to emphasize the importance of the modern era and that tradition is ongoing and does not just stop with the Fathers of the Church; secondly, I respected what has already been published, for example, *Journey with the Fathers*,[1] which is along the

---

1. E. Barnecut, ed., *Journey with the Fathers*, Year A, B, C (Hyde Park: New City Press, 1992-94).

lines of this book with a heavy emphasis on Church writers, and *Tradition Day by Day*,[2] readings for each day of the year from Church writers.

Lectio Divina

When we hear the word "reading," we immediately think of taking up a newspaper, magazine, or book and reading through it for information or for enjoyment. This is one type of reading. However, there is another type of reading in the Church's tradition, in which one reads not for information, although this may come with the reading, nor for enjoyment, although this can be present, but for the enrichment of the inner spirit. It is a type of reading that is a prayer in itself; you are (or seem to be) reading, but actually you are praying. The patristic texts in particular lend themselves to this type of reading because they are filled with quotes from scripture or with scriptural allusions. But some modern readings can elicit the same.

Thus, in reading such texts, you are feeding the inner spirit and you are praying. In addition, the texts prompt many beautiful thoughts, ideas, and prayers. One cannot just read the text and put it aside; the text stays with you and leads you to greater depths of thought and prayer. This is *lectio divina*—literally, divine or sacred reading.

A medieval writer in the book *Meditations of Saint Augustine* depicts well this notion of *lectio divina:*

> I love to raise the eyes of my heart to you, elevate my mind to you, and shape the affections of my soul to harmonize with you. I love to speak and hear and write and converse about you, daily to read of your glorious blessedness, and frequently to mull over in my heart what I have read of you. In this way I am able to turn from the passions and dangers and labors of this mortal and transitory life to the sweet coolness of your life-giving breezes and, when I so turn, to rest my weary head, even if only for a moment, on your bosom. It is for this

---

2. J. E. Rotelle, ed., *Tradition Day by Day* (Villanova: Augustinian Press, 1994).

purpose that I enter the pleasing fields of the sacred scriptures, there to find and pluck the fresh growth of its sentences, to eat by reading and digest by frequent meditation, and finally to gather them all into the deep storehouse of my memory.

How To Use This Book

One could pick up this book and read it from cover to cover, but I doubt if that person would derive much from that reading. The best way to use this book is twofold: First, you could read it in conjunction with the Sunday gospel in the proper cycle, that is, Year A, B, or C. Or, secondly, one who preaches could use it as background for a homily or sermon; others could use it in preparation for the Sunday celebration. The book could be used as a source of meditation either for each Sunday, or in preparation for the Sunday, or for some days during the year.

Inclusive Language

The readings range from the seventeenth to the twentieth centuries. Some are translations; others were written in English— English of different eras, a Cardinal Newman English to a Gerald Vann style.

Wherever possible, inclusive language has been the goal without detriment, however, to the meaning. At times it was easy, changing man to human being, men to men and women; at other times it was not so easy, and at times changes could not be made because the male or female (as in the case of Julian of Norwich) imagery was embedded in the text.

It is my hope that this florilegium of texts will help you to deepen your living of the gospel life and to provide you with moments of prayerful reading and revelation.

John E. Rotelle, O.S.A.

Readings

First Sunday of Advent

Gospel: Luke 21:25-28.34-36 Jesus said to his disciples: "There will be signs in the sun, the moon, and the stars. On the earth, nations will be in anguish, distraught at the roaring of the sea and the waves."

Commentary: P. T. de Chardin **F**rom the historical point of view, expectation of the parousia has never ceased to guide the progress of our faith like a torch. The Israelites were constantly on the watch for the Lord's coming; so too were the first Christians. Christmas, which one might think would have turned our minds toward the past, has actually carried them further forward into the future. For one moment the Messiah appeared in our midst, allowing himself to be seen and touched; then he vanished again, more luminous and mysterious than before, into the impenetrable depths of the future. He has come. Yet now, once again, we must go on expecting him more than ever. This time it is no longer a small chosen group that awaits his coming; it is the whole of humanity. The Lord Jesus will only come soon if we ardently long for him. The breakthrough of the parousia will be the result of a mounting flood of desire.

After Israel, we Christians have been charged with keeping the flame of longing alive in the world. No more than twenty centuries have passed since the ascension; what has become of our expectancy? Alas, we are disillusioned and suspicious, owing to the somewhat childish haste of the first generations of Christians combined with the mistaken perspective which made them believe that the return of Christ was imminent. The resistance of the world to good has shaken our faith in the kingdom of God. Perhaps a kind of pessimism, nurtured by an exaggerated idea of the fall, has led us to regard the world as radically and incurably corrupt. Consequently we have allowed the fire to die down in our hearts, and have let them grow numb within us. Where is the Catholic who, out of conviction, not by making conventional gestures, is as passionately devoted to spreading the hopes enkindled by the incarnation as are so many humanists to spreading the dream of a new secular city? We go on saying we are keeping watch in expectation of the master, but if we would really be honest we would have to admit that we no longer expect anything.

At all costs the flame must be revived. No matter what the price, we must rekindle in ourselves the desire and hope for the great future coming. But where are we to look for the inspiration for this revival? First and foremost, it is clear that we must seek it in an increase of Christ's own magnetic action on his members. But after that it will be in the growing seriousness with which we take the task our reflections have discerned: the task of preparing for the parousia and bringing it about. And where shall we find the greatest impetus to take this task seriously? In the discovery of a more intimate connection between the victory of Christ and the successful issue of human endeavor here below.

(*Le Milieu Divin*, 197-199)

Pierre Teilhard de Chardin (1881-1955), a priest of the Society of Jesus, was a scientist and theologian of unparalleled insight. Enlightened by a passionate love of God immanent in all things, and taught by a lifetime's meticulous study of geology, biology, and paleontology, he was brought to a vision of the universe's evolution toward its rebirth and transformation in a union of love with Christ, its "Omega-Point." This he explored in many of his writings, notably *Le Milieu Divin* and *The Phenomenon of Man*. His life was one with his teaching, absorbed in adoration, deeply aware of God's presence at all times.

Second Sunday of Advent

Gospel: Luke 3:1-6

Jesus said to his disciples: "There will be signs in the sun, the moon, and the stars. On earth, nations in agony, bewildered, by the clamor of the ocean and its waves."

Commentary: A. Rétif

John's stay in the desert was simply a burning expectation of the Savior. All the aspirations of the prophets and the just in Israel and the extremely fervent desire of the remnant of the holy people found in him their concentrated and almost explosive expression. Christ was certainly present to John in his solitude. And so, when he saw him with his eyes, his body did not quake. His faith was so lively and enlightened that he thought his eyes of flesh had seen him previously.

"A happy life," says Saint John Chrysostom, "is to scorn humans, seek the company of angels, flee the cities, and find Christ in solitude." Can better words be found to express at once both the focal point of his expectation and its realization? To find Christ is renouncing and abandoning all. This chaste man of faith had been the first to light his lamp and was like a person waiting. He was going to be the first to hear the shout in the night: *Behold, the Bridegroom comes.* The friend of the Bridegroom who gives his heart free rein is the first to leap with celestial joy when his beloved approaches. He was, it has been said, starving, but only for the One who was to come. Hence, he continues to be the model of every Christian and every missionary, whom each dawn and each sunset should find awaiting the return of the Son of Man anxiously, but without agitation, joining in that expectation of the last things, which we know throbbed in the heart of the early Christians.

To John the outline of the Messiah, which became clearer as he prayed and meditated on the sacred passages, was exceptionally real, tangible, and electrifying, and the whole world, contained in the Baptist's soul, was sighing for his presence far more ardently than the stag after living water.

16

We must not think that, because John the Baptist fled from the world, he was insensible to the ardent longings of his times. Just as a landscape has to be viewed from high above in order that one may appreciate its vast expanse, John had to leave the world to understand it and discover its immense distress; for, when viewed in God, things become extraordinarily clear and well defined. John, preceding his captain, the Messiah, was the first to test his strength with the devil and sense that the fate of a great number of souls depended on the outcome of the conflict. John was the first to take upon himself responsibility for the crowds whom he reached through the light of God without knowing them, and to pronounce the cry of pity for the sheep without a shepherd. Was he not already the shepherd of that immense flock that was to be led back to the fold of God? Was he not an invisible and unknown shepherd who would be imprisoned and decapitated in going to find his sheep?

John the Baptist is like all true contemplatives, monks, and saints in being eminently of his own times, which, however, he surpasses no matter what angle we view him from. Together with Mary, whose expectation preceded his own and was superior to it, he is the summit of the waiting for the Messiah, and he resembles those peaks on which the sun is already shedding its faint red rays when everywhere else night still reigns. If we are really to be men and women of our own times, do we not have to free ourselves from them in order to discover through God the whole of their inner meaning? So John, though he saw no men or very few of them, and did not move among the synagogues, alleys, and shops, bore his own times within himself in a more concrete and truer fashion than anyone else ever has borne them. It was in him and thanks to him that the whole history of the Old Alliance was going to end and permit him to show it its seed and its fruit.

(John the Baptist, 33-35)

André Rétif (1914-   ), born in Angers, France, studied for the priesthood at Angers' Grand Séminaire. In 1936 he entered the Society of Jesus and was sent, in due course, to complete his studies in Rome where he attained his doctorate in theology in 1948. Having a special interest in the Church's theology of mission he not only wrote on this theme but was himself sent on assignment to the Jesuit missions in Asia and Africa, working, among other places, in the Cameroons and Madagascar. His theological writings draw from this personal experience of the mission field.

Third Sunday of Advent

Gospel: Luke 3:10-18

All the people asked John, "What must we do, then?" John answered, "If anyone has two tunics, he must share with the one who has none, and the one with something to eat must do the same."

Commentary: J. Vanier

*I*t was into a confused and conflictual situation,
where anger and despair were smoldering,
that a man called John appeared.
He was a prophet.
There had been no prophets in Israel
for many years;
this made some people feel as if Israel
had been abandoned by God,
though others were still living in expectancy,
waiting and hoping for something to happen:
the end of the world?
the end of a world?
the coming of the Messiah?
The "one who is to come" to restore the Kingdom?

John dressed like a prophet,
in camel's hair,
not with the flowing garments of the Pharisees.
John ate like a prophet, locusts and wild honey.
John cried out like a prophet,
shouting the word of God with all its force and truth,
its simplicity and directness,
issuing severe warnings:
if people did not change their ways,
if they did not repent,
they would be punished,
eaten up by fire.

The end of the world?
The end of a world?

He cried out to the Pharisees and Sadducees:
"brood of vipers!"
warning them not to consider themselves an elite of God
but to change their hearts
and the direction of their lives.

(Jesus, the Gift of Love, 27-28)

Jean Vanier has devoted his life to caring for the wounded members of society, the poor, the handicapped, the elderly, prisoners, and the lonely. A firm believer in the importance of community, Vanier founded L'Arche, a community for mentally handicapped youths and adults in France. L'Arche communities have since been founded in many parts of the world, and Vanier himself has become an inspirational figure for people striving to live the gospel message of love.

Fourth Sunday of Advent

Gospel: Luke 1:39-45

Mary set out at that time and went as quickly as she could to a town in the hill country of Judah. She went into Zachariah's house and greeted Elizabeth.

Commentary: C. Houselander

Sometimes it may seem to us that there is no purpose in our lives, that going day after day for years to this office or that school or factory is nothing else but waste and weariness. But it may be that God has sent us there because but for us Christ would not be there. If our being there means that Christ is there, that alone makes it worthwhile.

There is one exquisite incident in Our Lady's advent in which this is clearly seen: the visitation.

And Mary rising up in those days went into the hill country with haste, into a city of Judah.

How lyrical that is, the opening sentence of Saint Luke's description of the visitation. We can feel the rush of warmth and kindness, the sudden urgency of love that sent that girl hurrying over the hills. *Those days* in which she rose on that impulse were the days in which Christ was being formed in her; the impulse was his impulse.

Many women, if they were expecting a child, would refuse to hurry over the hills on a visit of pure kindness. They would say they had a duty to themselves and to their unborn child which came before anything or anyone else.

The Mother of God considered no such thing. Elizabeth was going to have a child, too, and although Mary's own child was God, she could not forget Elizabeth's need — almost incredible to us, but characteristic of her.

She greeted her cousin Elizabeth, and at the sound of her voice, John quickened in his mother's womb and leapt for joy.

I am come, said Christ, *that they may have life, and may have it more abundantly*. Even before he was born his presence gave life.

If Christ is growing in us, if we are at peace, recollected, because we know that however insignificant our life seems to be, from it he is forming himself; if we go with eager will, *in haste*, to wherever our circumstances compel us, because we believe that he desires to be in that place, we shall find that we are driven more and more to act on the impulse of his love.

And the answer we shall get from others to those impulses will be an awakening into life, or the leap into joy of the already wakened life within them.

It is not necessary at this stage of our contemplation to speak to others of the mystery of life growing in us. It is only necessary to give ourselves to that life, all that we are, to pray without ceasing, not by a continual effort to concentrate our minds but by a growing awareness that Christ is being formed in our lives from what we are. We must trust him for this; because it is not a time to see his face, we must possess him secretly and in darkness, as the earth possesses the seed. We must not try to force Christ's growth in us, but with a deep gratitude for the light burning secretly in our darkness, we must fold our concentrated love upon him like earth, surrounding, holding, and nourishing the seed.

We must be swift to obey the winged impulses of his love, carrying him to wherever he longs to be: and those who recognize his presence will be stirred, like Elizabeth, with new life. They will know his presence, not by any special beauty or power shown by us, but in the way that the bud knows the presence of the light, by the unfolding in themselves, a putting forth of their own beauty.

(*The Reed of God*, 32-34)

Caryll Houselander (1902-1954) was born at Bath and became a Catholic while still a child. After receiving a general education she went on to study art, and later used her talents in many practical ways. World War II brought out especially her literary gifts as well as her compassion as a psychiatric therapist. Her works include: *This War is the Passion* (later revised as *The Comforting of Christ*), *The Reed of God, The Dry Wood, Guilt, The Stations of the Cross*, and *The Risen Christ*.

Christmas

Gospel: John 1:1-18

In the beginning was the Word: the Word was with God and the Word was God.

Commentary: Catherine of Siena

O depth of love! What heart could keep from breaking at the sight of your greatness descending to the lowliness of our humanity? We are your image, and now by making yourself one with us you have become our image, veiling your eternal divinity in the wretched cloud and dung heap of Adam. And why? For love! You, God, became human and we have been made divine! In the name of this unspeakable love, then, I beg you — I would force you even! — to have mercy on your creatures.

I am imperfect and full of darkness. Yet you, perfect and lightsome, have shown me perfection and the lightsome path of your only-begotten Son's teaching. I was dead and you revived me. I was sick and you gave me medicine — and not only the medicine of the blood that you gave to the sick human race in the person of your Son. You gave me as well a medicine against a hidden sickness I had not recognized, by teaching me that I can never sit in judgment on any person, especially on your servants. For I, blind and weak as I was from this sickness, have often judged others under the pretext of working for your hour and their salvation.

O immeasurably tender love! Who would not be set afire with such love? What heart could keep from breaking? You, deep well of charity, it seems you are so madly in love with your creatures that you could not live without us! Yet you are our God, and have no need of us. Your greatness is no greater for our well-being, nor are you harmed by any harm that comes to us, for you are supreme eternal Goodness. What could move you to such mercy? Neither duty nor any need you have of us (we are sinful and wicked debtors!) — but only love!

O eternal Father! O fiery abyss of charity! O eternal beauty, O eternal wisdom, O eternal goodness, O eternal mercy! O hope and refuge of sinners! O immeasurable generosity! O eternal, infinite Good! O mad lover! And you have need of your creature? It seems so to me, for you act as if you could not live without her, in spite of the fact that you are Life itself, and everything has life from you and nothing can have life without you. Why then are you so mad? Because you have fallen in love with what you have made! You are pleased and delighted over her within yourself, as if you were drunk [with desire] for her salvation. She runs away from you and you go looking for her. You clothed yourself in our humanity, and nearer than that you could not have come.

(*The Dialogue*, 50, 63, 325)

Catherine of Siena (1334-1380), Caterina di Giacomo di Benincasa, took a vow of virginity at the age of 7. At 18 she received the Dominican habit, when she began to live in solitude and silence in her room. After her "mystical espousal" to Christ in 1368 she rejoined her family and devoted herself to the service of the poor and sick, but continued her life of contemplation. In Pisa in 1373 she began her prolific letter-writing career. Through this, and her many travels, she sought to influence public affairs, to bring about a reform of the clergy and the return of the papacy to Rome from Avignon. Possessed of exceptional apostolic powers, especially in the reconciliation of sinners, she became the center of a group which regarded her as teacher and spiritual guide. As well as her "Dialogue," a spiritual work of considerable importance, we still have many of Catherine's letters. She was canonized in 1461, and declared a doctor of the Church in 1970.

Holy Family

Gospel: Luke 2:41-52

Every year the parents of Jesus used to go to Jerusalem for the feast of the Passover. When he was twelve years old, they went up for the feast as usual.

Commentary: G. Preston

Christian joy results from an option, from choosing to say that life has a meaning, even though the only name we can give that meaning is Jesus of Nazareth. All we have to go on is the word of God, that history is a history of redemption. He who came in Jesus of Nazareth will come again in him: that is the promise we have elected to live by. Joy results from the expectation of an end which will give meaning to all that precedes it, as the final movement of a symphony gives meaning to the opening chord and all that follows. Ultimately the coming again of Jesus is what our faith, hope, and joy stand or fall by. Meditating on Jesus' first coming offers a language for speaking of his second coming to bring in his kingdom of peace and justice.

The language of his first coming is a language of death and persecutions as well as of births and shepherds, wise men and carolling angels. It is a language of swords to murder babies, swords to pierce the heart of Mary; a language of the stony heart of Herod, and of stone for stoning Stephen. The loss of the child Jesus in the temple in Luke's gospel gives us, perhaps, the clue we need.

The passage is a most skillfully composed overture to Luke's presentation of the origins of the Christian faith in his gospel and the Acts of the Apostles, including all of his major themes. The loss takes place at Jerusalem at Passovertide, when and where the Lord was to be crucified. It *must be*, as the passion and death of Jesus must be. People involved in this incident fail to understand what he is about, seek him, and find him on the third day; as his own will do when he is killed and raised. At the finding there is the same sort of questioning: *Why were you looking for me — Why are you looking for the living among the dead?* In the infancy stories there is already present the passion, death, and resurrection of Christ: Jesus the child grows in stature, and in growing learns to die. The first coming is meant to prevent us from making too light of the second. We have to see the reality of the threat beneath which faith, hope, and joy lie. The story of Stephen, and the Innocents, and the three days' loss of Jesus teach us to interpret the very darkness of the world as a sign of Christ's coming.

(God's Way to be Human, 24-25)

Geoffrey Preston was born in Cheshire, England, the son of the local blacksmith. He was educated at the nearby grammar school and Durham University; it was during this time that he moved from Methodism through Anglicanism to the Catholic Church. A man of wide intellectual culture, he still retained his peasant simplicity and the habit of deep pondering on the word of God which he had learned as a Methodist. Entering the Dominican Order, he was made novice master after nine years. He died at the early age of 41.

Mary, Mother of God

Gospel: Luke 2:16-21   The shepherds hurried away to Bethlehem and found Mary and Joseph, and the baby lying in a manger.

Commentary: M. Thurian

The disciple whom Jesus loved can say of Mary that she is the Mother of Jesus and also his own mother; he realizes then the intimacy which unites him with Christ, his Lord and his brother. Mary, the mother of Jesus and his mother, is the person who is able to draw him closer to Christ, his Lord and his God. With him, she has been a witness of the last moments of the Crucifixion, she has heard the last words of Jesus, and has received the Spirit which He has transmitted to the Church. Mary is therefore for him, and, through him, for all the disciples, and for the Church which gathers about them, a very close sign of the presence of the Lord, a spiritual mother in the Christian community, the most venerated of all spiritual mothers found in the Church, the spiritual mother par excellence of the beloved and faithful disciples, of the brother of Jesus, which every Christian is called to be.

Immediately after the Ascension, we see, in the Acts of the Apostles (1:12-14), the group of the eleven, returning to Jerusalem and going into the upper room where they had habitually met with Christ. There they are to await the outpouring of the Spirit at Pentecost. *All these with one accord devoted themselves to prayer, together with the women, Mary, the mother of Jesus, and with his brothers.* Mary, the Mother of Jesus, is here integrated with the whole group of the disciples: the apostles, the women and the relatives of the Lord. With them, and in the midst of them, being of one heart and mind with them, she is assiduous in prayer, awaiting the great outpouring of the Holy Spirit which will open the missionary era of the Church. A type of Mother Church, she has no place of a ministerial or hierarchical kind, as have Peter, John, James, and the other apostles who are first named. She is mentioned among the women and relatives of Jesus. She is in the midst of the primitive Church, as a humble and praying example, as a handmaid of the Lord and of the Church. It is thus that she will receive the Spirit at Pentecost, in order that she may be fulfilled with the fullness of her vocation, in the very heart of the Church.

She appears indeed as the widow of the ancient Church *who sets her hope on God and continues in supplication and prayer night and day.* However, she is not alone; she has a son in the disciple whom Jesus loved; she is the spiritual mother par excellence in the midst of the faithful women who have followed Christ and who are always there. She is for the disciple, and for all the disciples, the type of Mother Church and the spiritual mother rediscovered in the Church. In the power of the Spirit, she will be able to transmit to the disciples and to the primitive Church all that she knew of Jesus, her beloved Son, and what she has so preciously guarded and pondered in her heart. She will be a humble bearer of the gospel of her Son, not in the same fashion as the missionary apostles, but in the manner of a discreet and loving mother, a human mother, the mother of the Son of God whom she has known better than anyone in the intimacy of His company, a spiritual mother of the disciples, to recall all that Christ said and did, and of whom she has been able to be a faithful and attentive hearer. By her faith, her hope, her charity, and her prayers she will be a spiritual mother of Mother Church, of whom she is the living and humble representative.

(*Mary, Mother of All Christians*, 170-171)

Max Thurian (1921-1995), born in Geneva, Switzerland, studied theology at the University of Geneva and then became a pastor. With Roger Schutz he founded the community of Taizé in France which is a famous ecumenical community of the religious life.

Second Sunday after Christmas

Gospel: John 1:1-18

In the beginning was the Word: the Word was with God and the Word was God.

Commentary: D. Dumm

*T*he divine Word took on a human nature so that the Father's love could be shared more fully with us, his beloved children. This love is intended to make it possible for us to live together in harmony and mutual support; it is intended to create vibrant and joyful human community, from the smallest family to the wide world of nations. God's final Word is, therefore, a word of love and God's purpose for creation is fulfilled when all that wonderful variety is filled with his love and lives in harmony.

John testifies that he and the other disciples "saw his glory," that is, they recognized the presence of God in the human person of Jesus. "Glory" in the Bible refers to any sense — perceptible manifestation of God's presence in our world — from the luminous cloud of the Sinai journey to the luminous love that shone through Jesus and touched his disciples. This glory was such as one would expect to see in the only-begotten, uniquely-beloved Son of God. The love of God transfigured the human nature of Jesus so that he glowed with inner confidence and freedom. In Jesus, the disciples saw what the love of God can do in a human being who receives it fully. Jesus thus becomes the final and perfect manifestation of "grace and truth" which were the attributes of God most cherished by Israel. "Grace" translates *hesed* which means merciful, gracious love and expresses Israel's first and deepest experience of God, for this was that wonderful impulse that caused God to choose them as his own people. "Truth" translates *emeth* which refers to the faithfulness and constancy of God in his loving of Israel. It was wonderful that God should have loved them; it was equally wonderful that he should not be fickle like humans but ever-faithful in his love for them. Jesus, in his loving unto death, is the perfect and enduring sign and guarantee of the Father's continued love and fidelity to all his children.

This revelation of the nature of God as One-who-loves is not presented as a statement of fact; it is expressed in history, in events. For nothing is more real and tangible than creation itself and this word is spoken to all in every moment of time. Israel enjoyed the special word of Torah spoken to all the world — a Word spoken to the heart more than to the mind. Those who dare to admit their hunger and who open their hearts to this Word will find their most personal history radically changed. Birth and death seem unreal in comparison to that event!

(Flowers in the Desert, A Spirituality of the Bible, 31-32)

Demetrius Dumm, O.S.B., is professor of New Testament at Saint Vincent Seminary in Latrobe, PA. Having studied at the École Biblique in Jerusalem and the Pontifical Biblical Commission in Rome, Father Dumm has also been a faculty member at the Institute of Formative Spirituality at Duquesne University and in the Intercommunity Program for Women Religious in southwestern Pennsylvania.

Epiphany

Gospel: Matthew 2:1-12   We have come from the East to worship the king.

Commentary: Thomas of Villanova

Epiphany proves how keen-sighted was the magi's faith. They had not yet seen the child perform any miracles or mighty works; they had not beheld him walking on the seas or raising the dead or giving sight to the blind; they had not experienced his wisdom or heard his teaching; and yet amid circumstances of extreme privation and lowliness they recognized the majesty of God and worshiped him. With acute spiritual discernment they pierced the veil of his flesh, and *behind our wall* they descried the king of glory. Wonderful indeed was the faith of that thief who prayed to God on a gibbet, but no less wonderful was that of the magi who worshiped God in a stable. The former recognized him hanging there; the latter knew him feeding at his mother's breast; the one knew him groaning, the others knew him crying; one confessed him when he was fastened with nails, the others when wound in swaddling bands; the thief acknowledged him as he departed this life, the magi as he entered it. Yes, but the thief had perhaps heard about Christ's deeds, while the magi had heard nothing about him worthy of remark.

Let us go too, my brothers and sisters, and seek the newborn Savior in the company of these wise men. Let us seek him no longer lying in a manger but enthroned in his kingdom, no longer wound in swaddling bands but crowned in glory and honor, no longer cuddled on his mother's breast but seated at the right hand of the Father, no longer consorting with animals but ruling amid throngs of angels. Let us seek him not by the rays of a star but by the light of faith. This will be our most reliable guide along the way; this will lead us by a direct path to our Lord and Savior, and reveal our king to us in the beauty of his majesty. Whoever you may be, if you thirst for the vision of the Lord of glory in eternal happiness, and if you truly long to reach the goal of your desire, do not turn your eyes away from this radiant star. Let us seek him in fervor of spirit, let us search diligently, let us search with perseverance. Let no temporal prosperity hold us back, nor the prospect of hardship and misfortunes deter us. No, rather let us hasten toward the glory of the heavenly kingdom through all life's vicissitudes and through its myriad ups and downs, trampling the deceitful allurements of this world underfoot.

We must not appear in his presence empty-handed, however. Let us offer gifts to our prince drawn not from our own treasure, but from his.

(Sermons, Epiphany, Sermon 1, 9-10)

Thomas of Villanova (1486-1555) abandoned an academic career to become in 1516 an Augustinian friar, and was made a prior before long. In 1533 while provincial he sent friars to the New World. After having declined the see of Granada, he was put under obedience to accept the archbishopric of Valencia which had been so neglected that he was excused from attending the Council of Trent. His time and money were devoted to the poor, the sick, and ransoming captives, so that he was called the Beggar Bishop, father of the poor. His many sermons had an influence on Spanish spiritual literature: particularly notable is one on the love of God, and in another he wrote of the conception of our Lady as most holy, without stain.

Baptism of the Lord

Gospel: Luke 3:15-16.21-22   A feeling of expectancy had grown among the people, who were beginning to think that John might be the Christ.

Commentary: J. Vanier

Many people came from Jerusalem
and all the surrounding districts
to be washed by John
in the waters of the Jordan,
confessing their unfaithfulness to God
and the evil they had done.
He called all to a change of heart.
He did not tell them to become Zealots
and to struggle through violence,
nor to obey the minute regulations of the Law.
He did not ask people to change externally —
— if they were soldiers or tax collectors
they should remain as they were —
but to change internally.
He cried out for repentance,
a change of heart.
He called people to compassion,
to share with the poor,
inspired certainly by the prophet Isaiah:
"Let those who have two tunics, give one away
to those who have none;
and let those who have food do likewise."
Above all,
John announced that "another is to come" after him;
John was but "a voice crying out in the wilderness"
attributing to himself
the words of the prophet Isaiah
to prepare the way of the Lord.
This other would baptize

not with water as he did,
but with the Holy Spirit and with fire.
John said he was not even worthy
to undo the straps of the sandals
of the one who was to come,
who was unknown to the leaders,
unknown to the people,
unknown even to him, John,
until the Spirit of God
in the form of a dove
descended upon this other.
This other was Jesus.
He came and knelt humbly before John
in the waters of the Jordan,
asking to be baptized by John
who recognized him then
as the Son of God,
the Messiah,
the one who was to come,
the one for whom he was called to prepare the way.
As he baptized Jesus
John heard a voice from Heaven saying:
"This is my Son, my Beloved,
in whom I am well pleased."
From then on John cried out:
"He must increase
and I must decrease."

(Jesus, The Gift of Love, 28-30)

Jean Vanier has devoted his life to caring for the wounded members of society, the poor, the handicapped, the elderly, prisoners, and the lonely. A firm believer in the importance of community, Vanier founded L'Arche, a community for mentally handicapped youths and adults in France. L'Arche communities have since been founded in many parts of the world, and Vanier himself has become an inspirational figure for people striving to live the gospel message of love.

First Sunday of Lent

Gospel: Luke 4:1-13

Filled with the Holy Spirit, Jesus left the Jordan and was led by the Spirit through the wilderness, being tempted there by the devil for forty days.

Commentary: E. La Verdière

In the first temptation, Jesus rejects the view that his divine sonship cancels out his humanity. Jesus is indeed Son of God, but he is also fully human and his messianic mission will in no way escape the limitations of the human condition.

In the second temptation, Jesus rejects the view that his mission is political. As messiah, he fulfills a divine mission and that mission is an act of worship. Had he sought political power, he would have played out his role in the worldly arena and rejected the total gift of himself to God, a gift consummated in his passion and death. In so doing, he would have been subject to the devil's illusory power.

In the third temptation, Jesus rejects the view that his divine sonship entails a special protection in the human sphere. Even for the messiah, any effort to circumvent human limits would be a divine affront and a betrayal of God's intention concerning human life. In accepting the passion, Jesus does not expect God to save him from death.

Jesus' response to the three temptations shows the Christian community how it should respond to its own basic temptations. In the Lukan historical context, these temptations have arisen in the areas of table fellowship, political relationships and persecution, all three of which are fundamental preoccupations in Luke-Acts.

Christians must not expect to be nourished automatically and for the simple reason that they are Christians. They must learn to situate the need for food among other life needs which are more basic. Christians should understand that their persecutions and political difficulties are normal for men and women bent on divine values. To greet political power with mere political power would be bowing to the enemy. Finally, Christians must not expect God to free them from the human condition. Trust in God should not be confused with the kind of foolhardy behavior which tries to control God and limit his freedom.

Luke's message is not limited to the passage's internal literary development and its thematic relationship to the remainder of Luke-Acts. The specific context in which the temptation account is present is also significant.

Unlike Matthew, Luke situated the temptations immediately after the genealogy of Jesus. The two are not unrelated. We have already noted how Luke insists on Jesus' humanity. Jesus is indeed Son of God, but his messianic mission unfolds within the human sphere. Such considerations move us beyond Israelite history and require that we view Jesus' temptations in terms of humanity's most basic struggle with evil. The conclusion of the genealogy, which associated Jesus with both Adam and God, had prepared us for this development. The problem in the genealogy, however, was to show how the son of Adam was also son of God. In the temptation story, the problem is the reverse, and Luke means to show how the son of God is fully son of Adam.

Jesus' mission marks humanity's complete victory over evil. Adam had fallen short of that victory. No ordinary son of Adam, Jesus rose to its challenge. Unlike Adam, he accepted the limitations of created humanity, and it is thus that he manifested the ideal of divine sonship. Jesus' divine sonship was revealed in his humanity, and his victory over evil was effected in his acceptance of creaturely limitations.

(Luke, 56-57)

Eugene A. La Verdière (1936-), born in Waterville, Maine, obtained his doctorate in theology at the University of Chicago after having studied at the University of Fribourg, Switzerland, and the Pontifical Biblical Institute in Rome, and at the École Biblique in Jerusalem. He is a priest of the Society of the Blessed Sacrament and writes articles and books on scripture.

Second Sunday of Lent

Gospel: Luke 9:28-36

Jesus took with him Peter and John and James and went up the mountain to pray. As he prayed, the aspect of his face was changed and his clothing became brilliant as lightning.

Commentary: Ä. Löhr

The Father gave Christ the resurrection and its brilliant light; he raised the servant who was faithful to him, his Son, to the height of his own glory. Throughout his journey, until the moment of his passion, the Lord was aware of the glory which awaited him at the end of it. When the traitor left the Upper Room, Christ said to his disciples, *Now the Son of Man has achieved his glory, and in his glory God is exalted; it is for God to exalt him in his own glory, and exalt him without delay.*

This unshakable certainty requires no exterior sign of assurance from the Father, for its own sake; but to strengthen the faith for his apostles for the time of the passion, the glory of the resurrection is anticipated for them to see for a moment on the mountain. To the faithful, the initiates, the Lord unveils, far from the crowd, his true essence, in order to give them certainty of the undying life which no earthly death can influence. Because they believe, their belief is to be strengthened by vision; but what they see will remain for them to be silent about, for the Lord wills to test the faith of the others first with his humble humanity. Only he who believes in the Son of Man is worthy to see God among men. On the cross spirits are to be divided before the incarnate Son of God can reveal his humanity.

In no other way is the vision of the transfigured Lord given to us today, and it is given to strengthen our faith. The Christ who lives on in his Church hides his glory beneath the veils of the mysteries. He hides the marvels of his power and grace beneath the symbolic words, signs, and deeds. The figure of the Church is a humble one; her sacraments, her sacrifice are lowly things, annoyance and silliness to the unbelievers, but for the faithful they are the power and the wisdom of God. In the sacrifice of the death of Christ, the glory of his resurrection and his heavenly existence is laid bare for those who have been initiated.

Today this transfiguration of the Lord is put particularly to the fore in the liturgical event. We see the glorification of Christ living in his Church. When she dies and rises with him in the mysterium, she reveals before the eyes of the faithful whom baptism has initiated into these things her God-filled being, her otherness. Just as in God's idea of the whole, she lived before time was, and will rule forever when it is no longer "between Father and Son and Holy Spirit," she makes her appearance today in the real but mystical presence of the liturgical celebration, with, or rather in, the glory of the Christ who was killed, but rose again.

With us, as with him before he had suffered, that glory is not continuously visible; only when we have borne the conformation to Christ throughout the whole of our earthly lives, and striven always more consciously to realize it, only when we have borne our share of the pain of Christ, to the last end in our body's death, will the full splendor of the risen and glorified Christ break out in us.

(*The Mass through the Year*, volume 1, 171-172)

Ämiliana Löhr (1896-1972) studied philosophy, literature, and history of art at Cologne. During her studies she felt a call to the monastic life, and in 1927 entered the Abbey of the Holy Cross, a new foundation of Benedictine nuns at Herstelle on the Weser, where she took vows in 1931. She was allowed to continue writing as far as the life in the Benedictine community permitted it. Unusually gifted, she published many essays, reports, and poems dealing with literary, contemporary, hagiographical, and liturgical themes. The most important theme of her writings, however, is the liturgy grounded in the theology of Odo Casel, O.S.B., which was practiced in her abbey. The intention of her first work, *The Mass through the Year* (*Das Herrenjahr*), was to make people personally and truly participate in Jesus' work of salvation. The book met with a lively response, had six editions, and was translated into English. Her books on the hymns and Holy Week are evidence of a liturgy practiced in everyday life; even after the reform of the breviary they are still a rich source of information for liturgists.

Third Sunday of Lent

Gospel: Luke 13:1-9

Some people arrived and told Jesus about the Galileans whose blood Pilate had mingled with that of their sacrifices.

Commentary: Paul VI

We cannot tear ourselves away from the dominant thought in the Church during this period of preparation for Easter. It is the thought of penitence, which contrasts with our habits and our mentality.

Can a Christian evade the law of penance? Christ uses strong terms: *Unless you repent, you will all perish.* Do not the need, the duty of penance arise from the intrinsic necessities of our being as fallen human beings? For such we are: we bear within us an atavistic disease, the consequences of original sin, which largely remain even after baptism; we are beings in need of moral supervision, atonement, expiation, that is, penance.

But now let us fix our attention for a moment on the interior aspect of penance, which is obligatory and possible for everyone, that known under the biblical term, *metanoia*, now almost in common use. Metanoia means conversion, repentance, inner change. It means a change of outlook. And it is the latter that is most important to change one's thought, ideas, way of judging oneself, to change one's conscience, from false to true.

In this liturgical period when the exhortation to metanoia, this inner penance, this reordering of our mentality and our morality, becomes pressing, we must ask ourselves with courageous sincerity: what must we correct in our secret, intimate, personal life? Once more Pascal's vivid sentence returns to our lips: "All our dignity consists in thought. Let us take care, therefore, to think well: this is the principle of morality."

To think well! Beloved children, remember that we must begin from this point. Bear in mind that it is not easy. Not just because of the mental effort it requires, an effort which, for the professionals of thought, philosophers, the seekers of speculative truth, may be extremely tiring and dramatic (let us recall the great converts) but also, and this applies to everyone, for the moral effort that is required in order to think well. To change one's erroneous and faulty mentality calls for humility and courage. To say to oneself: I have been wrong, requires considerable strength of character. The renunciation of certain fixed ideas one has, which seem to define one's personality: "That is what I think! I am free to think as I like! I belong to such and such an ideology, and no one will make me change my mind," really calls for a spiritual revolution, possible only for one who sacrifices what is most personal in him, his own opinion or conviction, to the truth. For those who are usually dominated by passionate instincts or by illicit interests, to change course in the direction of righteousness, virtue, religious spirit, is a very difficult and meritorious operation, an overwhelming attempt at renewal. To forgive an offense, for example, to overcome a capricious dislike, a point of honor, an opportunity to use violence can be an exercise of penance, along the right line of Christian love.

Anyhow, to change, to demolish, to renew — is it not in the nature of our revolutionary times? It all depends on what, how, and why things must be changed. Let us Christians be guided by the exhortation of Saint Paul, which the Church takes as her own: *Be renewed in the spirit of your minds.*

(Address of 1 March 1972)

Paul VI (1897-1978), born Giovanni Battista Montini, was ordained a priest in 1920 and in 1925 entered the Vatican Secretariat of State. In this service of the Church he filled several important posts until he was named archbishop of Milan by Pius XII on 1 November 1954. Montini was made a cardinal in December 1958, and elected pope on 21 June 1963. During his long pontificate he showed himself to be an intrepid pastor and a determined promoter of the decrees of the Second Vatican Council. In spite of opposition he firmly held the bark of Peter on its course into a new age.

Fourth Sunday of Lent

Gospel: Luke 15:1-3.11-32   The tax collectors and the sinners were all seeking Jesus' company to hear what he had to say, and the Pharisees and the scribes complained. "This man," they said, "welcomes sinners and eats with them." So he spoke this parable to them: "A man had two sons."

Commentary: John Paul II

Mercy—as Christ has presented it in the parable of the prodigal son—has the interior form of the love that in the New Testament is called *agape*. This love is able to reach down to every prodigal son, to every human misery, and above all to every form of moral misery, to sin. When this happens, the person who is the object of mercy does not feel humiliated, but rather found again and "restored to value."

The father first and foremost expresses to him his joy that he has been *found again* and that he has *returned to life*. This joy indicates a good that has remained intact: even if he is a prodigal, a son does not cease to be truly his father's son; it also indicates a good that has been found again, which in the case of the prodigal son was his return to the truth about himself.

What took place in the relationship between the father and the son in Christ's parable is not to be evaluated "from the outside." Our prejudices about mercy are mostly the result of appraising them only from the outside. At times it happens that by following this method of evaluation we see in mercy above all a relationship of inequality between the one offering it and the one receiving it. And, in consequence, we are quick to deduce that mercy belittles the receiver, that it offends the dignity of the human person.

The parable of the prodigal son shows that the reality is different: the relationship of mercy is based on the common experience of that good which is man, on the common experience of the dignity that is proper to him. This common experience makes the prodigal son begin to see himself and his actions in their full truth (this vision in truth is a genuine form of humility); on the other hand, for this very reason he becomes a particular good for his father: The father sees so clearly the good which has been achieved thanks to a mysterious radiation of truth and love, that he seems to forget all the evil which the son had committed.

The parable of the prodigal son expresses in a simple but profound way the reality of conversion. Conversion is the most concrete expression of the working of love and of the presence of mercy in the human world. The true and proper meaning of mercy does not consist only in looking, however penetratingly and compassionately, at moral, physical, or material evil: Mercy is manifested in its true and proper aspect when it restores to value, promotes, and draws good from all the forms of evil existing in the world and in humanity.

Understood in this way, mercy constitutes the fundamental content of the messianic message of Christ and the constitutive power of his mission. His disciples and followers understood and practiced mercy in the same way. Mercy never ceased to reveal itself, in their hearts and in their actions, as an especially creative proof of the love which does not allow itself to be *conquered by evil*, but overcomes *evil with good*. The genuine face of mercy has to be ever revealed anew. In spite of many prejudices, mercy seems particularly necessary for our times.

(Encyclical *Dives in misericordia* IV, 6)

John Paul II (1920-), born Karol Wojtyla, was ordained a priest in 1946, a bishop in 1958, made a cardinal in 1967, and elected Pope in 1978. Hewn from the colossus of Polish Catholicism, formed by the discipline of study and manual labor, his physical, moral and intellectual strength has been the rock on which the grace of God has built up the Church during a period of consolidation after Vatican II. His particular insights into the human condition, shaped by his interest in the theater, his gifts for poetry and play writing, and his study of personalist philosophy, have contributed much to the teachings of the Church.

Fifth Sunday of Lent

Gospel: John 8:1-11

Jesus went to the Mount of Olives. At daybreak he appeared in the Temple again; and as all the people came to him, he sat down and began to teach them.

Commentary: J. Vanier

After the Pharisees leave, the woman stands alone in front of Jesus. He says, *Woman, where are they? Has no one condemned you?* (He knows that nobody has, but Jesus likes to ask questions to which he already knows the answers.) He looks at her and smiles: *Has anyone condemned you?* She says: *No, Lord.* Jesus says: *Neither do I condemn you; go and do not sin again.*

It must have been a very deep meeting. If Jesus saw and loved the rich young man that he called forth, so at that moment did he love the woman. When Saint Augustine talks of this meeting, he talks of the kiss of mercy and misery. The woman becomes conscious that she is in front of the Liberator, because when Jesus looks at her and says, *Do not sin again*, he creates a relationship with her. She loves him for he has saved her, and she goes away with a new force in her being. She will not sin again, because there has been a communication between the eyes of Jesus and her being, the being of Jesus and her being, and a strength comes into her.

This woman taken in adultery, we know, represents each one of us, for the whole union of love with the Spirit is a union to which I can be faithful or not. The whole history of the people of Israel is symbolized in the story of the woman who became a harlot, in the sixteenth chapter of Ezekiel. She was poor and God took her up, covered her, clothed her, cleaned her, gave her life and brought her beauty. But she turned away from him and used this beauty and these gifts to attract men to her.

So it is with our civilization. There is no doubt that its deeper values have their source in the message of Jesus, which was propagated through time, from mouth to mouth, from Christian community to Christian community, from the rebirth at the moment of Pentecost. Our civilization bears many fruits of the message of Jesus, but we use many of these for ourselves, for our own possessions and our own power. And so the world is divided, and the rich people — or the vast majority of them — are the ones who have been baptized, and who call themselves Christians.

This is at the heart of each one of us, this meeting of Jesus with the woman taken in adultery. It is for us a very personal reality, for we have not been faithful to the quiet callings of the Spirit. We have turned away from the Lover and have used his gifts for our own power and glory.

We dare not hear this quiet whispering of the Spirit calling us forth, so that our hearts of stone may be touched and gradually transformed into hearts of flesh, opening ourselves to the wounded ones of the world, near or far, learning to love as God loves. This is the experience of the healing power of Jesus: we will be healed when we are conscious that we are adulterers, that we are filled with selfishness and have not followed this call.

(*Be Not Afraid,* 44-45)

Jean Vanier has devoted his life to caring for the wounded members of society, the poor, the handicapped, the elderly, prisoners, and the lonely. A firm believer in the importance of community, Vanier founded L'Arche, a community for mentally handicapped youths and adults in France. L'Arche communities have since been founded in many parts of the world, and Vanier himself has become an inspirational figure for people striving to live the gospel message of love.

Passion Sunday
Palm Sunday

Gospel: Luke 22:14-23.56   The passion of our Lord Jesus Christ.

Commentary: J. Pinsk   **W**hat is the meaning of Jesus' entry *into Jerusalem* amid the joyous shouts of the crowds? The cry of *hosanna!* that rings out during the entry procession was originally a typically messianic cry, the clamor for the messianic kingdom: "Bring good cheer! Bring salvation!" It is the same cry that rang out on the occasion of the great procession at the feast of Tabernacles, in which wreaths of foliage were carried.

The multitude accompanying Jesus' entry into Jerusalem evidently adopts the same ecstatic attitude, for Jesus is the Messiah-King, and as such they escort him into the city of God, in which the kingdom of God is to be proclaimed. Thus it is Pascha Domini, the passing, the passover, the entry of the Lord, but an entry accompanied by his people. And that is also the sense of our own procession of palms.

The palm branch handed to us makes us participants of the triumph of the King. The olive branch mentioned in the prayers in connection with the palm branch signifies the peace of the kingdom of God, a peace implying the absolute inviolability of the holdings of the kingdom of God, an inviolability assured by the victory of Christ. The favored multitude present at the entry of Jesus into Jerusalem in that fateful springtime long ago already grasped what was here being foreshadowed. Redeemed humanity, illuminated by the celestial light of faith, goes out to meet our Redeemer, who subjected himself to human sufferings and was about to close in mortal combat with death for the life of the whole world and triumph by his death.

That original entry into Jerusalem therefore already transcended the bounds of the purely historical. And when we march today in a procession of palms, we are also entering together with Christ the King, into the holy Jerusalem, whose transcendent reality is figured forth for us by the House of God. To the victor over death we cry, with the angels and the children of the Hebrews: "Glory, praise, and honor be to you, Redeemer, Christ the King."

(Cycle of Christ, 45-46)

Johannes Pinsk (1891-1957) was ordained in 1915 and was, successively, secretary to his bishop, religious instructor in Breslau, student chaplain in Berlin, and pastor in the Berlin suburb of Lankwitz. Pinsk came under the influence of the monks of Maria Laach, especially the abbot Ildefons Herwegan and the theologian Odo Casel. A spiritual leader in Berlin and a very popular speaker, Pinsk devoted his life to explaining the liturgy and bringing others to love it. His great concern was the image of the risen Christ and the Easter mystery, the experience of the Church as a worshiping community, and the consecration of the world through the sacramental life.

Easter Triduum
Evening Mass of the Lord's Supper

Gospel: John 13:1-15

It was before the festival of the Passover, and Jesus knew that the hour had come for him to pass from this world to the Father. He had always loved those who were his in the world, but now he showed how perfect his love was.

Commentary: G. Preston

What we are doing in the eucharist is profoundly involved with that coming. Whenever we eat this bread and drink this cup we placard the death of the Lord *until he comes*. Until he comes we are trying out for size what it will be like when he comes. He is food for the journey and the end of the journey is not yet. We pray for him to come, and still he comes only in signs, though the signs are his real presence. He comes only in signs, and so in the presence of those signs transformed into him, we tell God that we are still waiting in hope for the coming of our Savior Jesus Christ. Just at that moment when we are more than ever conscious that he is with us, we say such things as "Christ will come again" or "Lord Jesus, come in glory," or we say that we are doing this until he comes in glory. Yet we pretend that the end really is now: we eat together at the banquet God has prepared for us, and drink from the overflowing cup he has mingled and poured out for us. Again and again we wish peace to one another, that peace and unity which belong to the kingdom where the Lord Jesus lives for ever and ever. It is a prophetic sign, pretending for a while that he has come, roughing out his coming here and now.

We come thereby into a situation where what unites us is the word of God and one loaf and a common cup; this loaf and cup derive their significance from their relation to the death of Jesus to this world and his living to God. In fact they simply are this

Jesus dead to sin and alive to God, the one who is God's way of being man. This loaf and cup, which are the way that new and only true humanity is embodied in our world, are what make us a unity. They are what make us the body of Christ here and now, even as in the kingdom the unity of all mankind will be Christ, the Lamb of the Apocalypse with the marks of slaughter still upon him, the hanged man with the wounds that never healed but were glorified. Here and now we let ourselves be taken into that and live as though that were already so, just as in the liberated zones of occupied territories people now and again live for a while as though the liberation were final. By doing this we are set toward our destiny more fervently. We already feel ourselves at home in what is yet to be and more displaced in what still is. Here and now, with these very unrisen people with all their quirks and foibles and sins, many of them well known enough to me, I pretend that the end of all things which is the meaning of all things has come already. The eucharist is the sacrament of peace and unity between us. There we are, as Saint Thomas puts it in his hymn, "commensales," people who share a common table. There we are "companions," people who share one *panis*, one bread. The eucharist is *convivium*, a living together, the convivial experience of sitting at the one table and sharing the one bread and living the one life in the kingdom of God. At the eucharist we are playing at the future. If you want to find out what your real faith in the eucharist is, you should ask yourself not so much what it leads you to say you believe as what it makes you hope for.

(*God's Way to be Human*, 87-89)

Geoffrey Preston was born in Cheshire, England, the son of the local blacksmith. He was educated at the nearby grammar school and Durham University; it was during this time that he moved from Methodism through Anglicanism to the Catholic Church. A man of wide intellectual culture, he still retained his peasant simplicity and the habit of deep pondering on the word of God which he had learned as a Methodist. Entering the Dominican Order, he was made novice master after nine years. He died at the early age of 41.

Good Friday

Gospel: John 18:1-19.42   The passion of our Lord Jesus Christ.

Commentary: H. de Lubac

*T*he thoughts of a Christian may follow various attractions, but they are always drawn back, as by the force of gravity, to the contemplation of the cross.

The whole mystery of Christ is at once a mystery of resurrection and a mystery of death. Neither is complete without the other, and one word expresses both: the paschal mystery, that is to say, the passover. It is the transmutation of the whole being, implying a total separation from self which no one can hope to escape. The individual must renounce all natural values insofar as they are purely natural, even those which have made it possible to rise above one's personal limitations.

However authentic and pure the vision of unity that inspires and directs a person's activity, before it can become a reality it must be eclipsed. The mighty shadow of the cross must envelop it. Humanity must cease to regard itself as its own final end if it is to become one, for God is essentially a God who admits of no sharing, a God who must be loved without rival or not at all.

Nor is it possible to pass effortlessly from a natural to a supernatural love. To lose oneself is the condition for finding oneself. The rigor of this spiritual logic applies to humanity as a whole as well as to the individual, to my love of the human family and of particular people as well as to my self-love. The law of exodus is the law of ecstasy. We cannot avoid being part of the human race, but the human race as a whole must die to itself in every one of its members, so as to live transformed in God. The only perfect fellowship is a fellowship united in a common adoration. "The glory of God is a human being fully alive," but only by giving all this glory to God can the individual have access to life in total solidarity with others; in no other way can society be complete. Such is the universal passover which lays the foundations of the city of God.

Christ sustains the whole of humanity in his own person. Through his death on the cross that humanity renounces self-love and dies. But the mystery is deeper yet. He who bore all within himself was abandoned by all; the Universal Man died alone. Such was the climax of the *kenosis* and the completion of the sacrifice. This abandonment, even to apparent desertion by the Father, was necessary to effect reunion. Here we have the mystery of loneliness, of rending apart, becoming the one efficacious sign of gathering together into unity; a sacred sword reaching to the separation of soul and spirit only so that Universal Life may flow in.

"O you who are alone among the lonely, you who are all in all!"

To conclude in the words of Saint Irenaeus: "Through the wood of the cross the work of God's Word has become manifest to all; his arms are there extended to gather the whole human race together — two hands outstretched, since there are two peoples scattered over the whole earth. And because there is one only God above all and through all and in all, we see in the center of the cross one single head."

(*Catholicisme*, 206-207)

Henri de Lubac (1886-1991), after the study of law, entered the Society of Jesus in 1913 at Saint Leonary in Great Britain and taught fundamental theology at the Catholic Faculty of Lyon. With Cardinal Daniélou he founded in 1940 the series *Sources Chrétiennes*. From 1960 onward he was a member of various Vatican commissions in preparation for the Council, and after the Council continued to work on various commissions. He was created a cardinal by Pope John Paul II in 1983. He authored numerous books and articles, his book *Catholicism* being his masterpiece. Cardinal de Lubac died in 1991.

Easter Vigil

Gospel: Luke 24:1-12

"Why do you seek the living one among the dead? He is not here, but he has been raised."

Commentary: S. Bulgakov

On Easter eve, when the procession, having made its way round the church, stops in front of the closed doors, the minds of the faithful pass through an incalculably brief but spiritually significant moment as it were of perplexed, questioning silence: *Who shall roll us away the stone from the door of the sepulcher?* Will the sepulchre be empty because Christ is risen? When the doors open at the sign of the cross and we enter the brilliantly illuminated church to the singing of the triumphant Easter hymn, our hearts overflow with joy because Christ is risen from the dead, and the Easter miracle takes place in our souls. For we "see Christ's resurrection"; "cleansing our senses," we behold "Christ shining with light" and "approaching us like a bridegroom he comes forth from the tomb." We lose consciousness of time and place, transcend the confines of ourselves, and enter the timeless sabbath of *rest to the people of God.*

Earthly colors fade in the radiance of the white ray of Easter, and the soul contemplates only "the unapproachable light of resurrection": "Today all is filled with light, the heavens and the earth and the nether world." On Easter eve it is given to us to anticipate the life of the world to come, to enter the kingdom of glory, the kingdom of God. We have no words to express the revelation of the Easter vigil, for it is a mystery of the age to come, "the language of which is silence."

The perfect joy given us on that night, in accordance with the Lord's promise, is the Holy Spirit, who by the will of the Father reveals to us the risen Christ. The Holy Spirit is the actual joy of the Holy Trinity, the Father's joy in the Son and the Son's in the Father, and he is our joy in Christ's resurrection. In and through him we see the risen Christ, and in us he is the light of Christ's resurrection. Easter is for us not one among other holidays, but "the feast of feasts and triumph of triumphs." All the great holidays give us knowledge of the kingdom of God as manifested in his works in this world. But Easter is not a commemoration of a past event, it is a part of the world to come. Easter is an anticipation on the earth of the manifested glory for which Christ prayed to the Father in his high-priestly prayer — of the heavenly Jerusalem which in the fullness of time comes down from heaven to earth, according to the prophet's vision: *Arise, shine, O new Jerusalem, for the glory of the Lord is risen upon you.* Easter is eternal life consisting in the knowledge of and communion with God. It is righteousness, peace, and joy in the Holy Spirit. The first word of the risen Lord to the women was *rejoice* and to the apostle: *Peace be to you.*

(*A Bulgakov Anthology*, 178-179)

Sergius Bulgakov (1871-1944) was an Orthodox seminarian who turned to Marxist economics, but he gradually came through his economic and philosophical studies to reject Marxism and return to the study of theology. Married in 1898 and ordained a priest in 1918, he was forced from his university post by the Bolsheviks. One of the most original and gifted Russian theologians, Bulgakov became in 1925 dean of the Russian Orthodox Theological Institute of Saint Sergius in Paris, a position he held until his death.

Easter Sunday

Gospel: John 20:1-9

Early in the morning on the first day of the week, while it was still dark, Mary Magdalene came to the tomb.

Commentary: Thomas of Villanova

The holy, glad day of the Lord's resurrection has shone forth to-day to all. Let us rejoice, brothers and sisters, for *this is the day the Lord has made*: the mother of all good days, the origin of immortal life, the beginning of all our glory. Therefore on the day of this solemnity so venerable let us offer congratulations both to Christ and to ourselves. To Christ, I say, who, after the victory of the cross, brought back spoils from his enemies. To him God the Judge has awarded dominion over all things, on account of the agony of his harsh contest and the humility of his pure obedience, as he himself boasts with good reason, saying: *All authority in heaven and on earth has been given to me.* How glorious, how beautiful this day when he arose as victor from hell! How new, how wondrous a sight he offered to inhabitants of heaven in his flesh! A new kind of creature is revealed to the ages in his flesh, a race that had never been seen in the world from the beginning of time.

But for the same reason, congratulations should be offered to ourselves, because we now see the likeness of our future resurrection and gaze upon the sight of our hoped-for glory in Christ. It is our glory, brothers, that we consider, it is our beauty that we venerate; our resurrection has begun in Christ and will be brought to completion in us in his time. Our root now lives: undoubtedly we branches will also one day be brought to life. The vine has now appeared glorious: undoubtedly we vine branches will also be glorified. *I am the vine, and you the branches.* Does not the glorification of the vine and the life of the root look to and pertain to the branches? Surely much in every way, because whatever the root is like, so too the branches, and what is given to the root is preserved there for all the branches. In the life of the root is the sure hope of life for the branches. Christ, our root, arose: undoubtedly we also will arise. Let not the delay of our promised resurrection disturb us, brothers, since we have now received a pledge of this in our trunk. The head lives, thus life will be brought to the members.

In you, Lord Jesus, we all now live, in you we have risen up together, in you we have all already sat down at the right hand of the Father, as the apostle observes: *He raised us up with him and made us to sit with Christ Jesus in heavenly places.* It is conferred in virtue, which one day will be conferred in reality. Today a new Adam has appeared, formed not into a living soul, but into a life-giving spirit, the appointed father and origin of the future age, from whom a new progeny arise, not earthly and filthy, but heavenly and bright, so that, like their heavenly Father, they too might be heavenly children. Finally *the just will shine like the son in the kingdom of their Father.*

Christ arose from the grave today as the firstborn of the dead, and the glorious Christ anticipates the time of future regeneration. The renewed offspring of his children also follow this glorious one, *that he might be the first born among many brethren.* Among many brethren, I say, not among all, for although we all will rise because of him, we will not all be changed with him; but they will be changed who have borne his image in life, they will be transformed into the body of his brilliance who did not disdain to be transformed to the cross of his humility in this mortal life. Therefore Christ earned resurrection for all, but he will not bring to all the change of his resurrection, but only to whom it was prepared by his Father.

(*Sermons, Easter Sunday*, Sermon 1, 1-2)

Thomas of Villanova (1486-1555) abandoned an academic career to become in 1516 an Augustinian friar, and was made a prior before long. In 1533 while provincial he sent friars to the New World. After having declined the see of Granada, he was put under obedience to accept the archbishopriv of Valencia which had been so neglected that he was excused from attending the Council of Trent. His time and money were devoted to the poor, the sick, and ransoming captives, so that he was called the Beggar Bishop, father of the poor. His many sermons had an influence on Spanish spiritual literature: particularly notable is one on the love of God, and in another he wrote of the conception of our Lady as most holy, without stain.

Second Sunday of Easter

Gospel: John 20:19-31   In the evening of that same day, the first day of the week, the doors were closed in the room where the disciples were, for fear of the Jews. Jesus came and stood among them.

Commentary: G. Mendel

Christ's day of victory, Easter day, breaks the bonds which sin and death have imposed, and the human race rises up in strength with its Redeemer from darkness and chains to the broad heights of heaven, to the heavenly realm.

Jesus left aside unbelievers and Jews; he appeared only to the chosen apostles, attended only to true believers. These he instructed, admonished, and sanctified, in order to turn them into complete saints.

The resurrection of the Son of God not only removed sin and death from us; it also won for us his grace, which through the Easter sacraments of baptism and the eucharist is impressed and planted in the soul, elevates the soul's whole being, transforms it, and makes it truly divine. Like an Easter sun, this grace flows out far and wide from the Redeemer's tomb, pours forth into the entire world, into souls; it is the light that is brought into existence on the day of the creation of a different, more beautiful, sublime world and that never disappears. For this purpose the sacrament of penance was established in the night, the darkness, and new life and joy are given to darkened, saddened souls.

Christ's victory won for us the realm of grace, the heavenly kingdom. The Easter banner becomes the banner of heaven, flag of eternity that waves victoriously over the gates of the heavenly city, Jerusalem. Here there is change, there changelessness, constancy.

For forty days Jesus reveals his new life in the most wonderful appearances and proofs of his presence. He manifests the sublime existence of one who is glorified, who is exalted above this world.

But at the same time he deals with his disciples in so simple and intimate a way that they soon lose all fear and in turn deal very familiarly with him. He appears to individuals and groups, he speaks with them, eats with them, urges them to be convinced of the reality of his resurrection. Each of these many appearances of the risen Lord contains a wealth of instruction, edification, and consolation for all times.

They recognized him, saw that it was clearly his very self: his figure, his gestures, his face — he was the same in even the smallest details.

He uses his wounds as marks by which he may be recognized. He points to his hands, feet, side. He takes with him into his glory not gifts but the marks of wounds. By his sufferings, by his wounds is the Savior to be recognized. Signs of love, signs that love lasts forever. These large, wide wounds he takes with him into his glory as his choicest possession, a possession which he retains and at the same time shares with those who love him.

(Sermons Manuscript)

Gregor Mendel (1822-1884), born in the Moravian town of Hyncice, now the Czech Republic, entered the famous Augustinian monastery at Brno. While serving in the teaching apostolate and parochial ministry, he became interested in natural science. Through study he increased in knowledge in this area and began the study of hybrids and cross fertilization, thus commencing on his discovery of the laws of heredity which he published, but recognition of this discovery came after his death when scientists in 1903, working on the laws of heredity, recognized the importance and validity of Mendel's studies. On 30 March 1868 Gregor Mendel was elected abbot of his monastery, Saint Thomas. He continued work in his experiments until his death on 7 January 1884. He is considered the discoverer of the laws of heredity.

Third Sunday of Easter

Gospel: John 21:1-19

Jesus revealed himself again to his disciples at the Sea of Tiberias. He revealed himself in this way. Together were Simon Peter, Thomas called Didymus, Nathanael from Cana and Galilee, Zebedee's sons, and two other of his disciples. Simon Peter said to them, "I am going fishing."

Commentary: J. Mouroux

Redemptive unity is achieved in the resurrection, which is a mystery of universalization. As the Father's response, the resurrection completes the divine plan of universal salvation; as the irrevocable judgment of God, it envelops the whole world of sin in a blazing light either of reprobation or of salvation. As the wresting of Christ from the grip of death — *I was dead, and see, I am alive for ever and ever* — it sets him free from all "carnal" ties with the universe, to plunge him wholly into that divine glory which is the life-spring of humanity transfigured. As the definitive exaltation of the Son, the resurrection constitutes him in the inexhaustible fullness of his privileges as head, priest, and king of the whole human race, making of him that *quickening spirit* from whom springs eternal redemption, the new creation, the *today* of grace for all humanity, past, present, and future.

Unheard-of mystery of universal redemption! Christ has become the firstfruits of a world raised up, the mother-cell of a ransomed universe, being appointed henceforward the all-powerful advocate, the supreme mediator, God's saving power eternally at work, the man who holds concentrated in himself the power of indestructible life. Thus on the one hand Christ draws to himself the whole of humanity because he has experienced every aspect of human existence: all that is corporal by his striving, his labor, his tears, and his dying; all that is mental through his joy, his anguish, his loathing and terrible fear of death; all that is spiritual through his contemplation, his free offering, his faithful love, crucified and crowned. Since Christ descended into the black abyss opened up

56

by sin to emerge from it victorious, the darkest secret of the human heart can climb back into light with the Risen One. For the person touched by Christ, all except sin is capable of transformation and will be transformed in due time.

On the other hand, Christ draws the whole human race to himself so as to form one body, the germinal nucleus of the new world. He seizes on interpersonal relationships at their deepest level, at their psychological center, and in all their facets (dialogue, cooperation, association), following up each aspect (acquaintance, affection, work, culture, politics) so as to rectify, purify, and transform them. We ought to study this mediating action in the Church under its specific forms; but we can see that it is always the divine agape which is at work, effecting in Christ the transforming encounter of human with divine and of human beings with one another.

Finally, by this same movement the risen Christ draws to himself the universe as the body of his body. He does not transform it from within, but he uses it for his own purposes. Little by little he disposes it for the service of his kingdom. Throughout the time he has allotted to it, until the people of the resurrection becomes an accomplished fact, he draws creation in his wake, directing it through those creative mutations which will find fulfillment in a new heaven and a new earth.

(*Le mystère du temps*, 149-152)

Jean **Mouroux** (1901-1973), after studying at Dijon under Gabriel Brunhes, and finding particular inspiration in the works of Thomas Aquinas and Maurice Blondel, was ordained a priest in 1926. Throughout his priestly life he devoted himself to gaining an ever greater understanding of the human capacity for relationship with God. This theme, developed in strongly personalist terms, is seen in his first and arguably greatest work, *Sens chretien de l'homme* (1945). The truth in which he placed his faith was the person of Christ, the real communication of God. For most of his life Mouroux was a professor, first of apologetics, then of dogmatic theology, at Flavigny. He attended the Second Vatican Council as a *peritus*.

Fourth Sunday of Easter

Gospel: John 10:27-30

Jesus said. "The sheep that belong to me listen to my voice, I know them and they follow me. I give them eternal life."

Commentary: A. Vonier

The metaphor of shepherd and flock did service for the concept of a ruler and his people over and over again in the inspired literature of the scriptures and also in secular writings. Kings, in classical language, were spoken of as the shepherds of their subjects. Avoiding any terms that might have a political savor, Christ succeeded in making it clear to his contradictors that he would have the best and most faithful and most enthusiastic following any leader ever had. Moreover his following would be unassailable, superior to all hostile attacks: *My sheep hear my voice. And I know them: and they follow me. And I give them life everlasting: and they shall not perish for ever. And no man shall pluck them out of my hand. That which my Father has given me is greater than all: and no one can snatch them out of the hand of my Father. I and the Father are one.*

There can be no doubt as to the political meaning of these solemn utterances if we take the word political in the sense of the leadership of human multitudes. Christ declares himself to be such a leader and one that will never succumb, never disappoint his followers as had done so many who had risen in those days and led the people astray after themselves. In the last instance he appeals to his divinity, to his oneness with the Father, to explain the infallibility of his leadership. The Jews had asked him point blank the question whether he would be their leader: *It was winter, and the time came for the feast of the Dedication in Jerusalem. Jesus was walking in the temple area, in Solomon's Portico, when the Jews gathered around him and said, "How long are you going to keep us in suspense? If you really are the Messiah, tell us so in plain words."* On the lips of those men that query had only one meaning: "If you are the promised leader of the people, tell us plainly and act accordingly."

58

Jesus does not want to be their leader; he answers them: *You refuse to believe because you are not my sheep.* Yes, he is a leader, but not their leader; he has a following, but they are not that following; he has a people, but they are not his people.

(The People of God, 45-47)

Anscar (Martin) Vonier (1875-1938), born in Swabia, entered the Benedictine Order at Buckfast Abbey in 1889 and was clothed as a novice in 1893, receiving the name Anscar. He did brilliantly at his studies in Rome and was sent back to Sant'Anselmo as a professor in 1905. In the following year he was to have accompanied his abbot to Argentina but their ship was wrecked; Abbot Natter drowned and Dom Anscar was elected abbot in his place. He presided over the immense task of the rebuilding of the abbey church by the monks themselves and was a source of deep spiritual inspiration by both his personality and his books, which include: *The Personality of Christ, The Divine Motherhood, A Key to the Doctrine of the Eucharist, The New and Eternal Covenant,* and *The Spirit and the Bride.*

Fifth Sunday of Easter

Gospel: John 15:1-8

When Judas had gone from the upper room, Jesus said: "Now has the Son of Man been glorified, and in him God has been glorified."

Commentary: A. Hulsbosch

In reading the New Testament one is struck by the fact that love toward God is hardly mentioned. And if ever it is mentioned, it is immediately accompanied by the statement that there is another command *like to* the first; or at any rate it is pointed out to us that we must not think that we love God if we hate our neighbor. *If anyone says, "I love God," and hates his neighbor he is a liar; for he who does not love his neighbor, whom he has seen, cannot love God whom he has not seen. And this commandment we have from him, that he who loves God should love his neighbor also.* Here again we find the thought that nobody has seen God. The only possible way of meeting him is through his creatures, in this instance, our neighbors.

Although we do not see God, as is said elsewhere in the letter, yet we on earth can really know him. We know him in the love which is in us. *Beloved, let us love one another; for love is of God, and he who loves is born of God and knows God. He who does not love does not know God; for God is love.* There is on earth, then, no knowledge or love of God except by means of the creation in which we meet God. It is an experiential knowledge of God. In the love which we bear our neighbor, we experience the presence of God. God reveals himself to us in love, and this love is creative. Because love evokes an answer or is itself an answer, Christians who love one another on earth are the creators of each other, because they reveal God to each other. Especially is the love of our enemies a creative love.

The spring of this love lies in God, the invisible. He has made his love visible in Christ. *In this the love of God was made manifest among us, that God sent his only Son into the world, so that we might live through him. In this is love, not that we loved God but that he loved us and sent his Son to be the expiation for our sins.* The love of Christ for

60

humanity is the revelation of the love of God for humanity. It is the *love of God in Jesus Christ our Lord* (Rom 8:39). Therefore, if we will to encounter the love of God, then we shall only be able to reach this love in its revelation in Christ, in *the love of Christ which surpasses all knowledge.*

(*God's Creation*, 218-219)

Ansfried Hulsbosch (1912-1973), born at Zanvoort, Holland, joined the Order of Saint Augustine in 1932. He studied philosophy and theology at Nijmegen, was ordained in 1938, and received a doctorate in theology at the Angelicum in Rome in 1941. He also obtained a doctorate in scripture at the Pontifical Biblical Institute. From 1945 to 1965 he taught New Testament exegesis at the Augustinian seminary in Nijmegen and his Order's international college at Rome. After a long illness he died on 2 February 1973. Over the years he published many well-received articles on exegesis and theology as well as several books in the same field.

Sixth Sunday of Easter

Gospel: John 14:23-29

Jesus said to his disciples: "If anyone loves me he will keep my word, and my Father will love him, and we shall come to him and make our home with him."

Commentary: L. Lochet

There is a profound reason why the apparitions of Christ after his resurrection took on such a hidden and fugitive character: he had not returned to stay with the apostles in a visible and sensible manner, but appeared only to disappear. He came in visible form so as to accustom them gradually to recognize his invisible presence by faith. It was that invisible presence, more real by far than the other, that he had come to give to the world.

Jesus himself had foretold this mystery. Just as he had prepared his disciples for his passion and resurrection, he prepared them to be open to this new mode of presence. *I tell you the truth: it is to your advantage that I go away, for if I do not the Advocate will not come to you. But if I go, I will send him to you. I will not leave you orphans; I will come to you.* These promises of Jesus make it abundantly evident that the abiding of the Spirit in the heart is a way not simply of replacing Christ's own personal presence, but of restoring it, renewing it in the most intimate way. *I will come to you. I shall be with you, because I live and you will live also.*

This means sharing in the life of the Father and the Son in the Holy Spirit. The Father manifests himself in the Son. The Father and Son give themselves in the Spirit, so that the soul possesses the Three-in-One within her, rejoices in their presence, and shares their own life. This presence of Christ by the Spirit establishes the Church in unity and catholicity, for it was this that gave the apostles the courage to disperse and leave Jerusalem in order to confront a hostile world. Had not Christ himself promised: *I am with you always, to the close of the age?* But the apostles remain in unity, since it is also true to say that because of this divine presence they will never leave Jerusalem; they will always be united in her.

Leaving the empty and rejected temple, they carry within themselves a consecrated temple where the living God abides. They are upheld by the power of God, because they carry his Word to the world. This Word speaks through them and creates a new world. One night, in a vision, our Lord said to Paul: *Do not be afraid. Speak out and do not be silent, for I am with you.* The first Christians loved to recognize this dynamic presence of Christ in the martyrs; he was their strength in the most exact sense of the word. When the hour of trial came, it was Christ who fought, suffered, and triumphed in them. That is why they were so perfectly at peace. Death itself was the coming of Christ into them, an irruption of his own life. It was not so much that death cut them off from the world, as that it united them forever to the triumphant Christ. What the apostles took to the world was the presence of Christ within them; it was this presence of Christ extended to the ends of the earth that formed the Church.

(*Le fils de l'Èglise*, 127-131)

Louis Lochet (1914-) was a member of a pastoral team of Rheims, France, a professor of philosophy and moral theology at the seminary in Rheims, and a member of the team for continuing education for his diocese. He writes with an emphasis on gospel witness.

Ascension

Gospel: Luke 24:46-53

Jesus said to his disciples: "So you see how it is written that Christ would suffer and on the third day rise from the dead, and that, in his name, repentance for the forgiveness of sins would be preached to all the nations, beginning from Jerusalem."

Commentary: A. Boultwood

When our Lord ascended, and the cloud had caught him from sight, his disciples stood rooted there on the mountain gazing as though by straining their eyes they could keep him with them on earth. But this was not the intent of divine wisdom. *All at once two men in white garments were standing at their side. Men of Galilee, they said, why do you stand here looking heavenward? He who has been taken from you into heaven, this same Jesus, will come back in the same fashion, just as you have watched him going into heaven.* Divine providence ordained that the redemptive work of Jesus should not go through his visible presence on earth, nor that people should contemplate in this life the glorified humanity of the Word. His divine mission would continue through his invisible Spirit, and by the faith which his disciples would carry to the ends of the earth.

Yet not all the joy nor all the vision is taken away. The ascension is a kind of wonderful bridge between the first coming of the Lord and the second. At his second coming he will come in all the fullness of his glory, and he will gather his faithful into the brightness of his kingdom, the dawn of all. At his first coming he came in all the weakness and helplessness of a child, to redeem the human race and establish his kingdom through suffering and the cross. But at the ascension the gates of heaven open upon the world as the Son of God returns to his Father, and the cross he leaves on earth is enlightened by the heavenly radiance that streams down upon it, and angelic promise is given of his triumphant return to lead us home: *This same Jesus will come back. Alleluia.*

This is why the ascension of Christ leaves not lamentation, but joy. The Church does not mourn this departure: *And as they gazed upon him ascending into heaven, they said: Alleluia.* They had had a very brief glimpse through the opening gates of heaven, they had heard a snatch of the angelic melody. It is from them on the night of Maundy Thursday, in Gethsemane. Then the prophecy had been fulfilled: *And Jesus said to them, Tonight you will all lose courage over me; for so it has been written, I will smite the shepherd, and the sheep will be scattered;* and they had been left in terror and grief, and in the guilt of their denial. Now in the strength of their faith and in the Holy Spirit that would come upon them, they went forth to preach Christ crucified, rejoicing that they were found worthy to suffer for his name.

(Alive to God, 96-97)

Alban Boultwood (1911-) was born in Stamford, Connecticut, and entered the Benedictine Order in 1929 and was ordained a priest in 1939. He studied at Collegio Sant' Anselmo in Rome and also at the University of Edinburgh. He was abbot of Saint Anselm Abbey, Washington DC, from 1961-1975.

Seventh Sunday of Easter

Gospel: John 17:20-26

Jesus raised his eyes to heaven and prayed, saying: "Holy Father, I pray not only for these, but for those also who through their words will believe in me."

Commentary: P. Bernard

The final stanza of the prayer is almost no longer a supplication. It is rather an observation of that which is and of that which will be, enhanced by a contemplation of the justice of God. Jesus comes back down from heaven to earth. Anew, he summarizes his work and his mission, he regards the present situation of his disciples, he perceives their continuation in the future; he desires but one more thing, that the love of the Father might always incline itself upon them and he himself be ever in them. These last words express a total acquiescence: the soul of Jesus is breathed out therein, without a trace of fatalism, in the serenity of a perfect submission and of a filial abandonment. Such is, it seems, the profound significance of the divine attribute, somewhat unexpected, which Jesus here accords to the Father. *"Just Father,"* you who are capable of seeing everything and of scrutinizing the depths of everything, you who give to one and to the other what is coming to him, sanction this discernment of spirits which is effected in virtue of my name; it is true, the world has not known you, and this is an immense misfortune, a great sorrow; but there is myself, who know you so perfectly, and these men here, who in me have the revelation of you; I shall continue this revelation in such a way that you can forever discern them from the world, find yourself in them, take them into your friendship, and I myself be always in them.

This prayer is even to the end the prayer of a leader. At the moment of departing, he requests that his men might be able to form a unity with him, in truth, in charity, in the tranquillity of his establishment, for the most vast gathering together of and the greatest profit of mankind. This unity imitative of God cannot be

66

consummated except in God. The leader is quite ready to sacrifice himself for this: he offers himself as a priest. Still, the sacrifice is not signified except in a discreet and almost veiled manner as the means of arriving at the supreme ends. Yet it is sufficiently in view that the whole prayer be marked by it, the prayer of a high priest as much as that of a great leader.

The seal of eternity is imprinted upon the entirety of this uplifting of soul. We have a sign of it in the tenses of the verbs. Several of the latter are in the past; but it is a past situated outside of time and expressing a kind of divine predestination. Things are said as if they were seen in a present full of all the future and ready for eternity. The prayer appears under this aspect especially at the beginning and at the end: the glory and the task of this leader, of this priest, are shown as properly pertaining to an order of eternal realities. The gathering together of the children of God antecedes "his oneness" in eternity. A man who offers prayers of this dimension is more than a great man; one is in fact obliged to surmise that this is a Man-God.

(*The Mystery of Jesus*, 338-339)

Pierre Bernard, a ranking exegete and spiritual writer, has combined his talents in a justly heralded work about the Son of God: *The Mystery of Jesus*. Making use of the latest findings of modern scholarship together with a profound knowledge of human nature, the author has drawn a portrait of Jesus that has earned praise from critics and public alike; the work has been quickly translated into many other languages and has brought the mystery of Jesus home to countless modern readers.

Pentecost Sunday

Gospel: John 14:15-16.23-26 Jesus said: "If you love me you will keep my commandments. I shall ask the Father, and he will give you another Advocate to be with you forever."

Commentary: J. Moltmann

The gift and the presence of the Holy Spirit is the most magnificent and wonderful thing that can happen to us, the human community, all living beings and this earth. For present in the Holy Spirit is not one of the many good or evil spirits lurking about; rather it is God himself, the God who creates and gives life, who redeems and blesses. In the presence of the Holy Spirit the end of the history of guilt, suffering and death has begun.

And it shall come to pass afterward . . . says God, we read in Joel 2:28. And what the first Christians experienced at the first "Pentecost" according to Acts 2 took place during the first days of the new creation of the world: the pouring out of God's creative power and spirit that gives life eternally, a stormy wind and tongues of fire with divine breath.

"Pentecost," as Christians call this event, is thus not an appendix and also not an addition to "Good Friday" and "Easter." "Pentecost" is the goal of Jesus' death on the cross and his resurrection by God into the glory to come. Where the Holy Spirit is, God is present in a special way and we experience God in our lives that are thus quickened by a source out of the depths of our being. We experience life, healed and redeemed, complete and in its entirety, with all of our senses. We feel and taste, we touch and see our life in God and God in our life. There are many names for God the Holy Spirit. The most beautiful among them for me are the names "Comforter" *(Paraclete)* and "source of life" *(fons vitae)*.

In praying for the coming of the Spirit, those who pray open themselves for the expectation and let the energy of the Spirit flow into their lives. Even when humans can still only groan for salvation and in their groaning become silent, God's Spirit is already groaning in them and interceding for them. Praying and groaning for God's Spirit to come into this life of imprisonment and this devastated world come itself from the Holy Spirit and are its first signs of life.

The response to the prayer for the Holy Spirit is his coming and staying, his being poured out and indwelling in us. Whoever prays for the Holy Spirit to come to us, into our hearts, into our community and to our earth does not want to flee to heaven or be removed to the great beyond. He or she has hope for his or her heart, his or her community and this earth. We do not pray, "Let us come into your kingdom . . ." We pray, "Your kingdom come . . . *on earth* as it is in heaven." Magnificent, unbroken affirmation of life lies behind this prayer for the divine Spirit to come to us fragile and earthly human beings.

("Pentecost and Theology of Life," The Lambeth Lecture, Kings
College, London, 11 January 1996)

Jürgen Moltmann (1926-), born in Hamburg, Germany, received his doctorate in theology from the University of Göttingen. He was pastor of the evangelical church in Bremen, Germany, and then professor of theology at the University of Bonn, 1963-1967, and from 1967 professor at the University of Tübingen, Germany. He authored books and articles on various themes.

Trinity Sunday

Gospel: John 16:12-15

Jesus said to his disciples: "I still have many things to say to you but they would be too much for you now. But when the Spirit of truth comes he will lead you to the complete truth."

Commentary: H. Rahner

When we first hear the mystery of the Trinity proclaimed our reaction is amazement that the Triune God should have surrendered himself so completely to his creatures and revealed to them his most intimate and precious secret. But this is what he did, out of a love which the incarnate Christ calls "friendship" and theology calls "benevolence." I have told you all that I learned from my Father. As Saint Thomas Aquinas wrote: "Revealing our secrets to a friend is something that is characteristic of friendship. When our friendship with another is so close that our two hearts are as one, then whatever we reveal to our friend seems to remain in the depths of our own heart. That is why our Lord said to his disciples: *I shall no longer call you servants.*"

And so we ourselves are at the very heart of God in the Trinity, through his having revealed this secret to us whom he created. He revealed it because, in the words of Saint Ignatius of Loyola, he "wanted to draw us into the depths of his heart." He drew us into this community of the divine nature because otherwise we should never have been able to grasp and contain within ourselves the secret of God's heart.

So the trinitarian mystery becomes the prototype and inmost foundation of our own sanctification. We can never fully understand our state of grace nor God's whole plan of salvation without building on this trinitarian basis. The Church itself has done so in the classical formula of the Apostles' Creed.

The creed is based on the trinitarian statement of belief. In its simplest shape it has been preserved for us in the baptismal formula of an ancient Egyptian papyrus:

I believe in God the Father Almighty,
and in his only Son, our Lord Jesus Christ,
and in the Holy Spirit
and the resurrection of the body
in the holy Catholic Church.

The structure of the entire economy of salvation is presented here with wonderful clarity. Our faith proceeds from the Father who in God is the first beginning and blessed ending. The creed begins not with a profession of faith in one God (belief in one God was indeed taken for granted), but with the profession of faith in this one God as the Father of an only Son. And this Son is our Lord, who bore the earthly name of Jesus but is also the Christ anointed by the Spirit — the Spirit who is equally the God of my faith. And so the Father and the Spirit have come to us in Christ.

The resurrection of the body will prove this conclusively. We shall rise again because through Christ the Holy Spirit has brought the divine life of the Spirit to earth, bringing spiritual life to the community which for that very reason is called the Holy Church. Thus the Church is an earthly reflection of what the Spirit is in God.

The Church is our native country where we are safe, and where our sanctification is accomplished through Christ until the glorious resurrection of our spiritualized being "in the holy Church." The Church then is the mystic circle where the end joins the beginning. It leads us to our original source, the Father, who sent his Son to us to bring his children home — those children of his who have been called together in the Church. Thus in the Church we see the image of the Spirit who unites Father and Son in mutual love.

("Trinitas als Anfang und Ende des Unsichtbaren," 26-28)

Hugo Rahner (1900-1968), older and not as well known as his world-famous brother, was nonetheless a highly regarded theologian and historian in his own right. Born at Pfullendorf, Germany, he joined the Society of Jesus in 1919. After his ordination, he became a professor at Innsbruck University, and from 1949-1956 he was rector of the prestigious International College, the Canisianum at Innsbruck. Before his death he published books on a variety of subjects, including *St. Ignatius of Loyola, Our Lady and the Church, Greek Myths and Christian Mysteries*, and *A Theology of Proclamation*.

Corpus Christi

Gospel: Luke 9:11-17

Jesus talked to the crowd about the kingdom of God; and he cured those who were in need of healing.

Commentary: J. Hoffmeister

*A*s the living Father has sent me and I live because of the Father, so they who eat me will live because of me. The Lord promises everlasting life to those who eat his body and blood. But he wishes to forestall the objection which the Jews raise in another place: *Abraham is dead, and the prophets. Yet you say: "Whoever keeps my word shall live for ever"?* Therefore he now begins to show the source of the power that enables those who eat his body to live for ever: *As the living Father has sent me and I live because of the Father. . . .* He is saying: "The fact that I live and live for ever, and can never perish, is due to the Father; that is, I have received it from the godhead." Thus his humanity has everlasting life not of itself but from his divinity. *So they who eat me will live because of me.* That is: "They who are incorporated into me and have me abiding in them shall live for ever, not because of anything they do, but because they are united to me in an indescribable but real way, and are incorporated into me."

He goes on immediately to say: *This is the bread that has come down from heaven.* Do you desire, you wicked people of Capernaum, to eat heavenly bread? Well, then, *this is the bread that has come down from heaven*, the One whom the Father has sent to you, the One who has come down to us, yet has not left heaven. He is heavenly and everlasting bread; no wonder, then, that he does such marvelous things in us. *Your ancestors*, he says, *ate manna in the wilderness and are dead. Whoever eats of this bread shall live for ever.*

We have believed, then, that Christ has given us his real body as a food which incorporates us into him, so that we may live with him for ever. But lest this most holy food turn into a poison for us, we must be very careful not to become a source of distress for Christ and not to indulge in hatred of our brothers and sisters. Let us rather consecrate ourselves to Christ and our brothers and sisters and be ready even to lay down our lives for them. Listen to what Saint Augustine says: "Those who receive the mystery of peace and unity but do not maintain the bond of peace receive the mystery not for their profit but as a testimony against them."

(Sermons, Eucharist, fol. XLIV-XLV)

Johannes Hoffmeister, O.S.A. (?-1547) was numbered among the best defenders of the Catholic cause in southern Germany, especially by his numerous writings in defense of the faith. In 1545 he preached at the Diet of Worms. The needs of Germany kept Hoffmeister from attending the Council of Trent. He died at Günzburg, Germany, on 21 August 1547.

Sacred Heart

Gospel: Luke 15:3-7

Jesus spoke this parable: "What person among you with one hundred sheep, losing one, would not leave the ninety-nine in the wilderness and go after the missing one till he found it?"

Commentary: H. A. Vaughan

God has done many and admirable things to prove his love for us, and to excite us to love him in return. But it would be impossible to point to any act of God which speaks to us so eloquently, and so forcibly, and so personally of his love as the act by which he decreed to die for us.

We are, by nature, skeptical and suspicious. We find it hard to accept the most earnest assurances of affection. And we seldom rest satisfied with words, unless more tangible proofs are also forthcoming. It is easy to break forth into fine speeches, and to soothe the attentive ear with fair promises, but we seek far more certain evidence than that. And, like the true Lover of our souls, Jesus, rather than lose our friendship or afford us any excuse for doubting him, accedes to our most unreasonable demands, and adds to all his other proofs, the proof of personal service. To love when love involves no pain; to love when all is according to our desires, and when nothing thwarts us, is comparatively an easy matter; but the true test of love is sacrifice. And the greater the sacrifice is, and the more personal, the greater is the love that it manifests.

Here we learn more and more fully the full significance of the text, *The Good Shepherd gives his life for his sheep*. We must resolve to make the cross of Christ our constant companion, our *vade mecum*; yea, it should be to us an exhaustless book, in which we may read on forever, of a love which knows no bounds and which puts to shame all human love, and wherein we may ponder over and over again the measureless depths of pity, and mercy, and compassion to be found welling up from the Sacred Heart, as from a copious and overflowing fountain.

Surely, if there be any sense of gratitude in our composition, if there be any feelings of affection, and devotion, and zeal left within our soul, the contemplation of Jesus, our Love, crucified and dying for us, will arouse them, and infuse into them fresh vigor and strength. We shall take up the burden of life with renewed firmness and resolution in spite of its difficulties, and shall be ashamed to be soft, delicate and fastidious members of a thorn-crowned head; and will resolve to suffer with Christ here that we may reign with him hereafter; and will not refuse to wear his livery of pain, and trial, and sorrow upon earth, knowing that it is such who will approach nearest to him, and share more abundantly in all his joys in heaven.

(*Sermons*, 241.245)

Herbert A. Vaughan (1832-1903), born in Gloucester, England, was educated in England and Europe and became very involved in various societies. He founded the Mill Hill Missionaries, the Josephite Fathers, and the Franciscan Missionary Sisters of Saint Joseph. He was named Archbishop of Westminster in 1892 and was responsible for building Westminster Cathedral. Vaughan published many manuals of devotion and religious instruction.

Second Sunday in Ordinary Time

Gospel: John 2:1-12

There was a wedding at Cana in Galilee. The mother of Jesus was there, and Jesus and his disciples had also been invited.

Commentary: M. Ward

The miracle of Cana is linked with that of the Cross by many of the Fathers: water and wine in one — the good wine of the Gospels kept until the coming of the Son into the world — water and blood in the other. And both at Cana and on Calvary "the Mother of Jesus was there."

In a brilliant article on "Our Lady in the Gospels" Father Alexander Jones shows us the enigma of the scene of joy which opened Christ's ministry. "Son, they have no wine," says Mary— and Jesus begins by appearing to refuse a request that has not been made. Taking the mere words, Mary had asked for nothing—but she receives the refusal as meaning consent. *What is it to me and to you?* [What business is it of ours?] *My hour is not yet come,* our Lord said — and Mary tells the waiters to be ready to do whatever He tells them. All this, as Father Jones points out, is not literature, it is speech. In conversation between intimates there are phrases half-spoken, words which a look transforms, silences which are understood. The only thing we can say with certainty about Cana is that Christ advanced His "hour" in answer to His mother's unspoken prayer.

From Christ thus, at the beginning of his public life, giving Mary to man as the most powerful of intercessors, the mind flies to Christ upon Calvary giving her to man as the most loving of mothers. Both in joy and in anguish the Mother of Jesus was there.

But another frame encloses this gospel yet more perfectly, if we read the first chapter as it was read by Justin, Irenaeus, and Tertullian, and as textual criticism tends more and more strongly to read it today: for 1:13, not the plural but the singular: *He who was born, not of the will of the flesh or of the will of man but of God*. Referring thus, not to the spiritual birth of Christians but to Our Lord himself, this text would show John asserting the Virgin Birth at the beginning of his gospel — placing Mary there also as he places her at Calvary, and thus setting not his ministry only but his total human life within a framework of reference to his mother.

(*They Saw His Glory*, 265-266)

Maisie Ward (1889-1975), born on the Isle of Wight, England, grew up in a family with many eminent friends and visitors. In 1926 she married Frank Sheed, an Australian, and together founded a publishing house, Sheed and Ward. Their goal in establishing the publishing firm was to lift the awareness of Catholic readers. Besides lecturing, writing, and publishing, she was also actively interested in humane projects.

Third Sunday in Ordinary Time

Gospel: Luke 1:1-4; 4:14-21 — Jesus, with the power of the Spirit in him, returned to Galilee; and his reputation spread throughout the countryside. He taught in their synagogues and everyone praised him.

Commentary: A. Goodier

Jesus unrolled the scroll, and read where it opened, the beginning of the sixty-first chapter of Isaiah: *The Spirit of the Lord is upon me, because the Lord has anointed me to heal the contrite of heart.* He stopped reading and rolled up the book; he restored it to the attendant and sat down. He was strangely quiet, calm, and self-possessed. His manner held them all; every eye was fixed on him. Then firmly, as would speak a master in Israel who knew, winningly, as from one who would be a benefactor, the words rang through the silence of the synagogue: *This day this scripture is being fulfilled in your hearing.*

He had chosen for his text one of the tenderest, one of the most hopeful, of the prophecies of the Messiah. Elaborating it he spoke to them of meekness, of a contrite heart, of captives; as he spoke they knew that they themselves were included by him in these categories. He spoke as one who had lived with them in bondage and knew the weight of chains. Gently he spoke to them, as one who understood; sympathetically, as one who knew how hard it would be for them to bend; encouragingly, as to those who had already yielded to despair; hopefully, as one who pointed to a new horizon, and strength restored, and a future of bright things. Gracefully he drew them on, unconsciously they followed; under the spell of his attraction they were dumb; as they listened to his invitation, telling them that he was there to lead them, to teach them, to heal them, to set them free, to give them all their heart's desire if they would but take it, they did not know that even as he

78

spoke he had begun to cast his spell about them, and that they had but to yield to be entirely won.

The eloquence of Jesus! Founded on crystal sincerity, and unspeakable truth, and a sympathy that included every human heart, and a companionship that endured with them all; and behind it an authority which carried beyond argument, and compelled men to say that never did man speak as he spoke; it was not eloquence, it was much more — it was utter truth uttering itself, convincing by its own transparency, blinding and subduing by the brightness of its light, conquering beyond possibility of doubt every man of goodwill who hears it.

For a moment there was silence, the silence of the Eastern sky before the dawn. At length a head moved and the spell was broken. The men looked round; they cast enthusiastic glances at each other; there was admiration, and joy, and satisfaction to tears in their eyes and hearts as they woke from their trance and began to speak: *And all gave testimony to him, and they wondered at the words of grace that proceeded from his mouth.* Would that they could have remained like this, with the freshness of the morning dew upon them! But it was not to be. Their first impulse, almost irresistible, had been of admiration and surrender; now, as they looked at one another, the old tone revived, and they affected to be doubtful. They owned to the beauty of all that he had said, but memory was slippery, and criticism was sharp, and very soon they were able to forget it.

(*The Public Life of Our Lord Jesus Christ*, 131-133)

Alban Goodier, S.J. (1869-1939), born in Great Harwood, England, joined the Society of Jesus in 1887. After ordination to the priesthood he worked in London with students and then was sent to the University of Bombay, India, to help with the crisis there. He became Archbishop of Bombay in 1919. He resigned from the see in 1926 and dedicated himself to retreats, lectures, and sermons. His scholarly bent, simplicity, and deep piety are revealed in his writings.

Fourth Sunday in Ordinary Time

Gospel: Luke 4:21-30

Jesus began to speak in the synagogue, "This text is being fulfilled today even as you listen."

Commentary: R. Guardini

The sharpest criticism, the most impatient rejection of holiness is always to be found in the prophet's own home. How can we admit someone whose parents we know, who is "exactly like anybody else" to be allied with holiness? What, So-and-so, whom we've known all our lives, a chosen one! This is scandal, Jesus' most powerful adversary. It closes people's ears and hearts to his message, however joyful; arms men against the kingdom for which he stands. Danger of such scandal was closely allied to the person of Jesus. When John the Baptist sent his disciple to him from the dungeon to inquire whether he was the Messiah, the Lord answered with the same words he had used in Nazareth to identify himself and to proclaim the nearness of the kingdom: . . . *the blind see, the lame walk . . .*

In Nazareth, scandal, flickering since Jesus' very first words, now flares up. Then it glimmers hidden under the ash. At the end, its roaring conflagration closes over Christ's head: eternal revolt of the human heart against the bearer of its own salvation.

Scandal — source of the power that Jesus' enemies organize against him. They use any "reasons" for their hatred that they can find: that he heals on the Sabbath; that he dines with people of ill repute; that he does not live as an ascetic, and so on. The real reason is never given; invariably it is this mysterious, inexplicable impulse of the fallen human heart revolting against the holiness that is God.

Thus into the hour glowing with the fullness of holy beauty and truth slash the words: *Is not this Joseph's son?* and Matthew adds: *Is not his mother called Mary, and his brethren James and Joseph and Simon and Jude? And his sisters, are they not all with us? Then where did he get all this?*

Jesus forces the enemy to step from his ambush: You doubt me? You whisper: Why doesn't he work the miracles he has worked elsewhere here in his own city? Let me tell you! There I could work, because there they believed in me; but you do not believe. And why not? Because I am one of you! Beware, what happened to those nearest Elijah and Elisha will happen to you: their own people refused to believe and fell from grace, and the holiness which they denied was given to strangers!

But the hour is Satan's. From those who had just witnessed, amazed and moved, the grace and beauty of Jesus' words, a paroxysm of rage breaks lose. They thrust him out of the synagogue and through the streets of the city to the precipice of the hill on which it lies, to hurl him from it. Rejection of the kingdom's eternal, inexpressible abundance has become a living possibility. Already the cross stands waiting.

However, the hour in which *the power of darkness* has its will entirely has not yet come; the incident is turned into a demonstration of spiritual power. The strongest things are the stillest. The scene in the temple before Easter, when Jesus single-handed overthrows the tables of the money-lenders and drives the crowds of bartering pilgrims from his Father's house, is striking enough. But what occurs here in Nazareth is an ever greater proof of spiritual force. The excited mob, infuriated by neighborly hate and general demonic hysteria, surrounds Jesus, drives him up the hill to the brink of the precipice and tries to force him over it to his death. Suddenly, in the thick of the clamor and chaos, the quiet words: *But he, passing through their midst, went his way.* No return of violence for violence. Soundlessly, effortlessly, divine freedom walks right through the seething mob, its irresistible force bound by nothing on earth but its own *hour*.

(The Lord, 45-47)

Romano Guardini (1885-1968), born at Verona in Italy, grew up in Mainz and was ordained in 1910. Ten years later he was admitted to the faculty of divinity at Bonn. In 1923 he became professor of dogmatic theology at Breslau and in 1945 professor of philosophy at Tübingen. His books were widely read by the laity and had great influence especially on the younger generation. They include: *The Lord, The Faith and Modern Man, The Living God,* and *Sacred Signs.*

Fifth Sunday
in Ordinary Time

Gospel: Luke 5:1-11

Jesus was standing one day by the Lake of Gennesaret, with the crowd pressing round him listening to the word of God, when he caught sight of two boats close to the bank. The fishermen had gone out of them and were washing their nets. He got into one of the boats — it was Simon's.

Commentary: G. Vann

Do you remember our Lord's words to Simon: *Launch out into the deep*? There is always a temptation to think of religion as something added on to the main business of life, like an annex to a building; but if we think of it like that we miss its whole meaning, and the meaning and adventure of life. It is not something added on to life, but an entirely new dimension into which life is plunged as you plunge into the sea. The temptation is always to live on the surface of life: to concern ourselves with the jobs and joys that every day brings without bothering our heads about what lies beneath it all; but that means not living fully at all, because it means that there is a lack of depth in our lives. No; *launch out into the deep*, our Lord tells us; it can be a frightening thing, the first time you plunge into the sea, because you are in a new strange element; but if you go on you forget the fright and enjoy the thrill, the sense of freedom; and the strange element becomes friendly and buoyant even while it remains immense.

That is what religion is meant to be like: it means not just knowing more things than you otherwise would, but knowing something underneath all things, knowing the secret heart of things, because you know the Presence, the Love, that is in and about all things. It means plunging into the divine life as a diver plunges into the sea. That is why our Lord said that he came that we might have life and have it more abundantly; it you plunge into this element you escape from the narrow confines of the selfish and the shallow, and move into immensity. It can be frightening; but again he tells us, *Fear not;* and there is always his hand to sustain us and encourage us as he sustained and gave courage to Peter when he was sinking.

You remember how Simon answered our Lord: *Master, we have labored all night and have taken nothing.* That is what you may often feel about your prayer. But you must go on as Simon did: *At your word I will let down the net;* and then you remember Saint Luke tells us that when they had done this they enclosed a very great multitude of fishes. Sometimes people fail because they are trying to pray in a way for which they are not suited; but usually that kind of dryness as it is called, the sense of terrible effort and lack of results, is a necessary stage in the adventure, the discovery of a way of teaching us really to love the God we are finding and not just (as it might otherwise be) the joy of the finding.

Nobody expects an adventure to be nothing but effortless ease. This is the greatest adventure of all, since it is what, through God's mercy, reveals to us life in its fullness; it is worth the effort.

(*The High Green Hill*, 7-8.10)

Gerald Vann (1906-1963) was educated by Dominicans and in 1923 entered the Order. He was ordained six years later. His studies took him first to Rome and then to Oxford. He returned to Laxton as a member of a teaching staff and afterward became headmaster and superior of the house. He was a prolific author with a special gift for conveying profound truths in a very readable way to a wide public. He was interested in the moral problem of war, and as early as 1936 founded a Union of Prayer for Peace.

Sixth Sunday
in Ordinary Time

Gospel: Luke 6:17.20-26

Jesus came down with the Twelve and stopped at a piece of level ground where there was a large gathering of his disciples with a great crowd of people from all parts of Judea and from Jerusalem and from the coastal region of Tyre and Sidon who had come to hear him and to be cured of their diseases. Then, fixing his eyes on the disciples, he said: "Blessed are you who are poor: yours is the kingdom of God."

Commentary: A. Bloom

We must remember that all we possess is a gift. The first beatitude is one of poverty, and only if we live according to this beatitude can we enter into the kingdom of God. This beatitude has two aspects. First, there is the very clear fact that we possess nothing which we can keep, whether we want to or not; it is the discovery that I am nothing and that I have nothing — total, irremediable, hopeless poverty. We exist because we have been willed into existence and brought into existence. We have done nothing for it, it was not an act of our free will. We do not possess life in such a way that it is impossible for anyone to take it away from us, and all that we are and all that we possess is ephemeral in this way. We have a body — it will die. We have a mind — yet it is enough for one minute vessel to burst in a brain for the greatest mind to be suddenly extinguished. We have a heart, sensitive and alive — and yet a moment comes when we would like to pour out all our sympathy, all our understanding for someone who is in need, and at that moment there is nothing but a stone in our breast.

So, in a way, we can say that we possess nothing because we are masters of nothing which is in our possession. And this could lead us, not to the sense of belonging to the kingdom of God and rejoicing in it, but to despair — if we did not remember that although none of these things are ours in such a way that they cannot be taken away from us, yet we *are* in possession of them. This is the second aspect of the beatitude. We are rich, and everything which we possess is a gift and a sign of the love of God and the love of men, it is a continuous gift of divine love; and as long as we possess nothing, love divine is manifested continuously and fully. But everything we take into our hands to possess is taken out of the realm of love. Certainly it becomes ours, but love is lost. And it is only those who give everything away who become aware of true, total, final, irremediable, spiritual poverty, and who possess the love of God expressed in all his gifts. One of our theologians has said "All the food of this world is divine love made edible." I think this is true, and the moment we try to be rich by keeping something safely in our hands, we are the losers, because as long as we have nothing in our hands, we can take, leave, do whatever we want.

This is the kingdom, the sense that we are free from possession, and this freedom establishes us in a relationship where everything is love — human love and love divine.

(Beginning to Pray, 14-15)

Anthony Bloom (1914-), Metropolitan of Sourozh, born Andrew Borisovich Bloom in Lausanne, Switerzerland, was educated at the Sorbonne, became a doctor of medicine before taking monastic vows in 1943 and became a priest of the Russian Orthodox Church in Paris in 1948. In 1960 he was ordained archbishop of Sourozh and then became in 1965 Metropolitan and Patriarch of Moscow and All Russia in Western Europe. He lectured in various parts of the world and authored many books on prayer and the spiritual life.

Seventh Sunday in Ordinary Time

Gospel: Luke 6:27-38

Jesus said to his disciples: "I say this to you who are listening: Love your enemies, do good to those who hate you."

Commentary: G. Savonarola

Have mercy on me, O God, according to your great mercy. Not according to the world's mercy, so pitifully small, but according to your own great, immense, incomprehensible mercy, far exceeding all sins put together — according to that mercy whereby you so loved the world as to give your only Son. What greater mercy could be imagined, what greater love? Henceforth who could ever despair, who would not have confidence? God made himself a human being like ourselves, and has been crucified for us. Therefore have pity on me, O God, according to that great mercy which moved you to deliver up your own Son for us and through him to blot out all the sins of the world, enlightening the whole human family by his cross and restoring in him everything on earth and in heaven. Wash me, Lord, in his blood, enlighten me by his humility, reinstate me by his resurrection.

Have pity on me, God, not according to your lesser mercy. Your lesser mercy brings alleviation to bodily ills, but your great mercy grants remission of sin and raises the penitent by grace over all that is greatest on earth. According to this great mercy have pity on me, Lord, so as to convert me to you, wiping out my sins and justifying me by your grace.

Your mercy, Lord, is that abundance of pity that has always made you look on the needy with tenderness. Mary Magdalene comes to your feet, good Jesus, washes them with her tears, dries them with her hair; you pardon her and send her away in peace — that, dear Lord, is one of your mercies. Peter denies you, protesting with an oath that he does not know you; one look from you and he weeps bitterly. You pardon him, confirming him as prince of the apostles — another example, Lord, of your mercy. The thief on the cross is saved by a single word. Paul, at the time a rabid persecutor, is filled with the Holy Spirit as soon as you call him. Such, Lord, are your mercies.

Time would fail me if I tried to count them all. The number of your mercies equals the number of men, women, and children justified by your grace. No one can boast of his own achievement. Let all the just appear together, both those on earth and those in heaven, and let us ask them in your presence if it was by their own power they were saved. With one heart and one voice all will answer: Not to us, Lord, not to us, but to your name give the glory, because of your mercy and your faithfulness.

(Savonarola's Last Meditation in Prison, 33-35)

Girolamo Savonarola (1452-1498), a Dominican, who in 1491 was prior of the famous monastery at Saint Mark in Florence, Italy, was an avid reformer and spoke against church abuses. He was loved by the people, but not appreciated by the authorities because he criticized their way of life. He met his tragic end in 1498.

Eighth Sunday in Ordinary Time

Gospel: Luke 6:39-45

Jesus told a parable to his disciples: "Can one blind man guide another? Surely both will fall into a pit? The disciple is not superior to his teacher; the fully trained disciple will always be like his teacher."

Commentary: S. Kierkegaard

For every tree is recognized by its own fruit. It may well be that there are two fruits which very closely resemble each other; the one is healthful and good-tasting, the other is bitter and poisonous; sometimes, too, the poisonous fruit is good-tasting and the healthful fruit somewhat bitter in taste. In the same way love also is known by its own fruit. If one makes a mistake, it must be either because one does not know the fruit or because one does not know how to discriminate rightly in particular instances. For example, one may make the mistake of calling love that which is really self-love: when one loudly protests that he cannot live without his beloved but will hear nothing about love's task and demand, which is that he deny himself and give up the self-love of erotic love. Or a man may make the mistake of calling by the name of love that which is weak indulgence, the mistake of calling spoiled, whimpering, or corrupting attachments, or essential vanity, or selfish associations, or flattery's bribery, or momentary appearances, or temporal relationships by the name of love. There is a flower called the flower of eternity, but there is also, remarkably, a so-called everlasting flower which, like perishable flowers, blooms only at a certain time of the year — what a mistake to call the latter a flower of eternity! And yet it is so deceptive at the moment of blossoming. But every tree is known by its own fruit. So also is love known by its own fruit and the love of which Christianity speaks is known by its own fruit—revealing that it has within itself the truth of the eternal. All other love, whether humanly speaking it withers early and is altered or lovingly preserves itself for a round of time — such love is still transient; it merely blossoms. This is precisely its weakness and tragedy, whether it blossoms for an hour or for seventy years — it merely blossoms; but Christian love is eternal. Therefore no one, if he understands himself, would think of saying of Christian love that it blossoms; no poet, if he understands himself, would think of celebrating it in song. For what the poet shall celebrate must have in it the anguish which is the riddle of his own life: it must blossom and, alas, must perish. But Christian love abides and for that very reason *is* Christian love. For what perishes blossoms and what blossoms perishes, but that which *has being* cannot be sung about — it must be believed and it must be lived.

(*Works of Love*, 25-26)

Søren Kierkegaard (1813-1855) resided all his life in the large family dwelling in central Copenhagen, where he was prominent as a literary figure. An unhappy love affair, quarrels with other writers and, in his last years, with the Church — all documented in lengthy journals — make up the story of his life. Graduated in theology, he put off taking orders (Lutheran); still, an overriding sense of what the gospel can mean to those who embrace it with faith and love led him to sandwich in between his various poetical and philosophical writings a number of spiritual books.

Ninth Sunday in Ordinary Time

Gospel: Luke 7:1-10

When Jesus had come to the end of all he wanted the people to hear, he went into Capernaum. A centurion there had a servant, a favorite of his, who was sick and near death. Having heard about Jesus he sent some Jewish elders to him to ask him to come and heal his servant.

Commentary: K. Rahner

The gospel story emphasizes the wonder and astonishment of Jesus at the centurion's faith. One might almost say that the centurion's attitude is matched by a similar attitude on the part of Jesus, but on a divine scale. He also is the child of his people. He also respects the limitations imposed on his earthly life, for he knows that he is sent primarily only to his people, to the lost sheep of the house of Israel. And in Saint John's gospel he says that *salvation comes from the Jews*. Hence: *Truly, I say to you, not even in Israel have I found such faith.* This practical demonstration, evidently genuine and spontaneous, that outside the people of God, outside the covenant, outside what was for hundreds and thousands of years the special field of God's activity, there existed more faith, more loyalty, more respect for what was good and valuable, this single demonstration is broadened by Jesus to the extent of saying that *many will come from east and west and from north and south* — as Saint Luke adds — *and sit down with Abraham and Isaac and Jacob in the kingdom of God* at that everlasting divine banquet, while the sons of the kingdom, those who thought that their descent from Father Abraham would give them a right to this eternal kingdom of God, are thrown into the outer darkness, *where there will be weeping and gnashing of teeth.*

Does all this not have some meaning for us? It is certainly possible that we could fail to put a high enough value on the grace of Christ found in the Church, but it is also possible that we could fall into the opposite error of thinking that we alone are the chosen ones, we who are inside, the sons and daughters of the kingdom. Jesus by his example is saying this to us: You must be the kind of people who will not hesitate to recognize the truth, to recognize goodness, honest, virtue, loyalty, courage, wherever they appear. You must not be party men. You must see the light wherever it shines. It may be anywhere, without prejudice to the truth of the Church. We know from our faith that God's grace is not confined to the visible Church of Christ, that God's grace comes and goes through all the alleyways of the world and finds everywhere hearts in which supernatural salvation is wrought through this faith and this grace. So we Catholics should not fall into the mistake of thinking that, because we are the children of the true Church, there can be no divine grace or love except in our hearts. We must be told again and again what this gospel tells us, that the children of the kingdom can be among those cast out, while others who did not seem to be chosen will come from the four corners of the earth and be numbered among the elect. The grace of the true Church should make us feel humble in two ways. First because we must admit to ourselves that we are perhaps not all that we could be if this grace were fully alive and true in us. Secondly, because it brings us no certain guarantee of election. So let us follow the example of the Lord and be open and generous in recognizing whatever is good, whatever is noble and active and admirable and alive, wherever it may be, in recognizing that grace can work also outside the visible Church. Let the grace we have received make us all the more humble and so prepare us to enjoy its fruits in eternity.

(*Biblical Homilies*, 19-21)

Karl Rahner (1901-1984), a Swabian by birth, entered the Society of Jesus in 1922 and was ordained ten years later. After completing his studies at Freiburg and Innsbruck he was appointed to the theological faculty of Innsbruck in 1936. In 1949 he became a professor of dogmatic theology and in 1964 was appointed to a professorship in Munich. As a theological editor his name is associated with Denziger's *Enchiridion Symbolorum* and also with the *Lexikon für Theologie und Kirche* and *Sacramentum Mundi*. He was a peritus at Vatican II and the many volumes of *Theological Investigations* testify to his tireless labor as a theologian. Etienne Gilson drew attention to Rahner's "combination of intellectual modesty and audacity." A theologian of penetrating insight, he was also without doubt a man of God.

Tenth Sunday
in Ordinary Time

Gospel: Luke 7:11-17

Jesus went to a town called Naim, accompanied by his disciples and a great number of people. When he was near the gate of the town, it happened that a dead man was being carried out for burial, the only son of his mother, and she was a widow.

Commentary: L. Boros

*J*esus turned to those who could see no way out of their troubles and lived under a crushing burden of toil, affliction and oppression, who were of no significance to anyone and were destined by a cruel fate simply to disappear from this world without a trace, along with all their sorrows and sufferings. He became an associate of such people, the *anawim*, Yahweh's poor, whose most glorious song his own mother had sung: *My soul magnifies the Lord, and my spirit rejoices in God my Savior, for he has regarded the low estate of his handmaiden. . . .* He felt himself drawn to those whose life was spent in bitter failure, who had no other riches but God. He was drawn also to those who supposed that they could not even expect help from God, to those who were sick within, to sinners.

But this desire to help the oppressed was not a passing emotion; it was the central theme of his doctrine of God and of salvation. The heart of God is full of mercy. God does not rejoice at those who count themselves "righteous," but at the sinner who repents, who is like the lost sheep that is found, or the silver coin for which the woman searches diligently until she discovers it again. God is the father who keeps watch for his lost son and, when he sees him coming at a distance, hurries to meet him, embraces him and kisses him. The Lord is like the vinedresser, who leaves even the fig tree that has produced no fruit, and patiently waits until it bears fruit at last.

Jesus made this demand of his followers: *Be merciful, even as your Father is merciful.* Mercy is an essential condition of the kingdom which he desired to set up; for only the merciful can expect mercy of God. He repeated the sublime demand of the prophet Hosea: *I desire mercy, and not sacrifice.* This mercy must be tender and gentle. It should bring close to me those in misery whom I come across on my way through the world, and make them my "neighbors," just as the man whom the robbers on the road to Jericho attacked, stripped, wounded and left for dead, was accepted as a neighbor by the Samaritan. I must have pity on those who are in my debt, and I will be judged solely by the mercy I have shown, a mercy that, perhaps unconsciously, I may have shown to Jesus himself in my brother who was suffering. So the preaching of Jesus constantly returns to the theme of mercy. He showed by this how deeply he was moved by the distress of the suffering and the needy.

Luke shows this in a deeply affecting passage. One day Jesus came into a small village; a man who had died was being carried out, the only son of his mother, who was a widow, and a great crowd from the village was with her. When Jesus saw her, he had compassion on her and said to her, *Do not weep.* The bearers stood still. He came and touched the bier, and said, *Young man, I say to you, arise. And the dead man sat up, and began to speak. And he gave him to his mother.* The reaction of the crowd was one of fear and astonishment. Luke says expressly: *Fear seized them all.* But from start to finish, the structure of this event is that of human mercy. There is nothing about it that seems strange to us. The mother's suffering directly affected Jesus, and aroused in him a deep emotion of love, due to his direct identification with the helpless person. This inward feeling expressed itself at once in effective help. Jesus used his miraculous power, restored the dead man to life and gave him back to his mother. If we had such powers at our disposal, we would act in exactly the same way.

(*God Is with Us*, 60-61)

Ladislas Boros (1917-), born in Budapest in 1917, was ordained in 1957. He attended Jesuit houses of study in Hungary, Austria, Italy, and France, and also the University of Munich, where he received his doctorate in philosophy. He was dean of studies of philosophy and religions in the theological faculty of the University of Innsbruck. He gained international fame with his work in the area of the theology of death. Among his works are: *The Moment of Truth, Pain and Providence, Meeting God in Man,* and *God Is with Us.*

Eleventh Sunday in Ordinary Time

Gospel: Luke 7:36—8:3

One of the Pharisees invited Jesus to a meal. When he arrived at the Pharisee's house and took his place at table, a woman came in, who had a bad name in the town. She had heard he was dining with the Pharisee and had brought with her an alabaster jar of ointment.

Commentary: S. Schneiders

When we look at the sinners in the gospel we do not find them to be unmitigatedly evil. The sinners often did very good and beautiful things. In fact, if they had not habitually observed at least the most essential demands of the law they would probably have been in Roman prisons, not listening to Jesus, for murder, robbery and the like are also against the civil law! The Samaritan, the publican praying in the temple, the sinful woman who washed Jesus' feet, the dying thief on the cross, were all, in fact, behaving as the law commanded. What characterizes the sinners, in other words, is not their breaking of the law, which might not have been any more serious or frequent than the sins of the righteous in any given case, but the fact that they had, in a certain sense, "given up on the law" as a source of salvation or as a criterion of acceptability to God. Most of the sinners were simply simple folk of the land who had neither the leisure nor the learning to be knowledgeable in the law and who found themselves frequently outside it even when they were not choosing evil for motives of pleasure or profit. Such people had only two choices, to despair of their salvation or to develop a humanly groundless and stubborn hope that God would find a way to save them in spite of the fact that they were and always would be sinners.

It is well worthwhile to explore the spirituality of such people. They are those who believe in salvation but do not believe that it will come from the law. They are "lawless" in a certain sense. They are "outside the law," not because they habitually violate it but because it is useless for them to try to keep it integrally. They are those for whom the law functions to teach them that they are truly helpless, in need of a salvation which the law cannot provide, as Paul says. In other words, the law can never absolutely assure them that they are doing God's will, that they are "good." They must do their best but trust only in God. They cannot demand rewards or approval from God as their just deserts. They can only receive salvation, if at all, as a free and undeserved gift.

Such people are involved in a kind of existential humility; the only prayer that they can say with any conviction is that which magnifies God for God's utterly prodigal mercy and that which implores God's mercy on themselves. And, by the same token, such people can never condemn anyone else, however much another may look worse than themselves, because they have given up the norm by which to decide who is righteous. If they do not declare themselves either condemned or saved on the basis of their own relationship to the law, how can they make any such declarations about anyone else? To despise or condemn another is to assume the status of the righteous and to lose one's claim to being among those for whom Jesus came. This is the lesson Jesus gives to the righteous Simon who condemned the repentant woman.

(*New Wineskins*, 160-161)

Sandra M. Schneiders, a member of the Congregation of the Sisters, Servants of the Immaculate Heart of Mary of Monroe, Michigan, since 1955, is associate professor of New Testament and Christian Spirituality, a staff member of the Institute for Spirituality and Worship at the Jesuit School of Theology, and a member of the doctoral faculty in scripture and spirituality at the Graduate Theological Union in Berkeley, California. She received the S.T.L. from the Institut Catholique in Paris and the S.T.D. from the Gregorian University in Rome.

Jerome Seripando (1491-1563), born in Naples, Italy, entered the Order of Saint Augustine in 1507 and became noted at an early age for his knowledge and for his administrative abilities. He was elected prior general of the Order in 1539 and traveled extensively to the Order's house to combat Lutheranism that had penetrated the Order and to work for the return of his religious. He was involved in the Council of Trent, first as a counselor of the Legate, Cardinal Cervini, and later as Papal Legate. Seripando goes down in history as one of the most influential of the council fathers.

Twelfth Sunday in Ordinary Time

Gospel: Luke 9:18-24

One day as Jesus was praying alone in the presence of his disciples, he put this question to them, "Who do the crowds say I am?" And they answered, "John the Baptist; others Elijah; and others say one of the ancient prophets come back to life."

Commentary: J. Seripando

The teaching on patience in tribulation could not be more clearly explained than Christ explained it when he was asked by the sons of Zebedee, his apostles, or by their mother, to grant them the first places in his kingdom. He replied by asking them whether they could drink the chalice he would have to drink. It is as though he were saying: You must first reflect on whether desire for my kingdom is so much a part of you and has taken such a deep hold on you that you are ready to suffer and bear, patiently and freely, the adversities and torments of this world in order to win that kingdom.

He explained it again when he likened the kingdom to a nobleman who wanted to conquer a kingdom in a far distant land and before leaving called his servants together and gave each a large sum of money, bidding them do their best with it and show some profit. Having won his kingdom and returned home, he wanted to see how diligent his servants had been and what profit they had made. He rewarded the diligent ones according to the amount they had gained. There was one, however, who through negligence and laziness had made no gain; from him the master took the money and left him unrewarded.

This nobleman is Jesus Christ who went off to heaven in order to bring the reign of God to its completion. But his intention is that with the money, that is, the gifts and graces given to them, his faithful servants should daily struggle and endure great labors and pass through great trials for the completion of the reign of

God. When Jesus Christ returns for judgment, these servants will be well rewarded and have a large share in the crown and riches of that blessed kingdom. But those who hold on to the gifts and graces God has given them through Jesus Christ but fail to use them and to be diligent and labor for the glory and completion of this reign will have no share in that kingdom because it has no share in them. They will not be crowned because they have not suffered.

Dear children, open your mouths with me, look up to heaven, and say with hearts raised to your heavenly Father: *Your kingdom come!* If you seek eternal glory in the kingdom of God, know that you will not enter into it unless the grace that is your guide to that glory enters into you. If you seek Jesus Christ, the blessed One, who sits on high at the right hand of the Father, you cannot reach there unless he first descends into your hearts in order to dwell there and later to judge the living and the dead. If you seek heaven, do not think you can enter it unless the virtue of humility first enters your souls. If you seek the reward, you must be called to labors and, if your labors are to deserve a reward, you must also be justified. If you seek the crown, you will never obtain it unless you are first adorned with fortitude, constancy, and patience so that you can struggle courageously.

Look to yourselves, then, and be clear on all these points when you say: *Your kingdom come!* The petition is one, but you are asking that five gifts come to you from the kingdom of God so that you may enter that kingdom. The first is the grace and favor of God. The second is union with Jesus Christ, the blessed Son of God, and his coming in judgment. The third is the virtue of humility, which God loves and exalts beyond every other virtue. The fourth is to be called and justified by God so that he may then lead you on the road to his glory and reward you with eternal life. The last is the strength and patience you need for the struggles and persecutions of this life, so that you may attain to the crown of peace, where you will see the immortal and invisible King of the ages, the one true God, being duly honored and glorified by the angels and the souls of the blessed. We pray humbly and constantly that we too may by God's grace be accepted into their company. Amen.

(Le prediche salernitane, Sermon 7, 161-162)

Thirteenth Sunday in Ordinary Time

Gospel: Luke 9:51-62

As the time drew near for Jesus to be taken up to heaven, he resolutely took the road for Jerusalem and sent messengers ahead of him.

Commentary: A. de Mello

God's kingdom is love. What does it mean to love? It means to be sensitive to life, to things, to persons, to feel for everything and everyone to the exclusion of nothing and no one. For exclusion can only be achieved through a hardening of oneself, through closing one's doors. And the moment there is a hardening, sensitivity dies. It won't be hard for you to find examples of this kind of sensitivity in your life. Have you ever stopped to remove a stone or a nail from the road lest someone come to harm? It does not matter that you will never know the person who will benefit from this gesture and you will receive no reward or recognition. You just do it from a feeling of benevolence and kindness. Or have you felt pained at the wanton destruction, in another part of the world, of a forest that you will never see and never benefit from? Have you gone to some trouble to help a stranger find his or her way though you do not know and will never meet this person again, purely from a goodheartedness that you feel within you? In these and so many other moments, love came to the surface in your life signaling that it was there within you waiting to be released.

How can you come to possess this kind of love? You cannot, because it is already there within you. All you have to do is remove the blocks you place to sensitivity and it would surface.

The blocks to sensitivity are two: Belief and Attachment. Belief — as soon as you have a belief you have come to a conclusion about a person or situation or thing. You have now become fixed and have dropped your sensitivity. You are prejudiced and will see the person from the eye of that prejudice. In other words, you will cease to see this person again. And how can you be sensitive to someone you do not even see? Take just one or two of your acquaintances and lift the many positive or negative conclusions you have arrived at and on the basis of which you relate to her/him. The moment you say so-and-so is wise or is cruel or defensive or loving or whatever, you have hardened your perception and become prejudiced and ceased to perceive this person moment by moment, somewhat like a pilot who operates today with last week's weather report. Take a hard look at these beliefs, for the mere realization that they are beliefs, conclusions, prejudices, not reflections of reality, will cause them to drop.

Attachment — how is an attachment formed? First comes the contact with something that gives you pleasure: a car, an attractively advertised modern appliance, a word of praise, a person's company. Then comes the desire to hold on to it, to repeat the gratifying sensation that this thing or person caused you. Finally comes the conviction that you will not be happy without this person or thing, for you have equated the pleasure it brings you with happiness. You now have a full-blown attachment; and with it comes an inevitable exclusion of other things, an insensitivity to anything that isn't part of your attachment. Each time you leave the object of your attachment, you leave your heart there, so you cannot invest it in the next place you go to. The symphony of life moves on but you keep looking back, clinging to a few bars of the melody, blocking your ears to the rest of the music, thereby producing disharmony and conflict between what life is offering you and what you are clinging to. Then come the tension and anxiety which are the very death of love and the joyful freedom that love brings. For love and freedom are only found when one enjoys each note as it arises, then allows it to go, so as to be fully receptive to the notes that follow.

(*The Way to Love*, 81-84)

Anthony de Mello was a Jesuit priest and the director of the Sadhana Institute of Pastoral Counseling in Poona, India. He is the author of *Sadhana, The Song of the Bird, The Heart of the Enlightened, Taking Flight, Wellsprings*, and *Awareness. The Way to Love* is a never-before-published collection of the last meditations written by Anthony de Mello before his untimely death in 1987.

Fourteenth Sunday in Ordinary Time

Gospel: Luke 10:1-12.17-20   The Lord appointed seventy-two others and sent them out ahead of him, in pairs, to all the towns and places he himself was to visit. He said to them, "The harvest is rich but the laborers are few."

Commentary: L. Cerfaux

When the disciples return from their apostolic tour full of enthusiasm, they will tell our Lord: *The devils fled before us! Yes*, answers the Lord, *I saw the conquest of the kingdom of Satan; but do not rejoice so much at that. The true reason for your joy is that your names are written in heaven.*

The apostles are the first to benefit from the kingdom of God. How could it be otherwise? Those who established the kingdom establish it first in themselves.

According to God's principles an apostle, because he is an apostle, is saved, chosen, already established in heaven. In the measure in which we share in the mission of the apostles worthily, we are already saved. Our salvation is measured by our gift of self to our apostolic vocation, which includes our salvation.

Thus we may forget about our personal salvation and center our life on this one desire: that the kingdom of God be established fully, that it take in all people, ourselves included. By our apostolic work and our cooperation with God our names are written in heaven.

The apostolic mission continues, always the task of human beings in a hurry, completely occupied by the kingdom of God. Our task is to save souls, and the most souls possible. *The kingdom of heaven is like the head of a household who goes out early in the morning to hire workers for his vineyard*. He keeps on hiring them until the eleventh hour.

Thus God continues to hire apostolic workers, first the twelve, then the seventy-two. After Pentecost came the great horde of workers in the vineyard: Saint Peter, Saint Paul, the whole history of the Church. God will hire workers for his vineyard forever, until the end of time.

We are the hired hands, and it is the great joy of our lives. People are unhappy because they have no task to take up their attention. They search ceaselessly, and even end face to face with themselves, terrified at their own mediocrity.

Our vocation is to work in the kingdom of God, and such is our mission. There are so many troubles in the world! There are physical troubles — which some day may be overcome. But moral troubles — who bothers about that? Disoriented lives, lack of ideals, deliberate denial of all ideals, the dreadful absence of God — who cares about that?

It is our job. We must not wait for someone else to do it.

We are beginning the mission of the apostles all over again, as if nothing had ever been done. But in the kingdom of God one can never say that nothing has been done.

Let us obey our Lord to the letter. Let us not stop, not greet anyone along the way.

Let us not listen to the voices which want to slow us down, the doubts which weaken our enthusiasm for the labor of an apostle. "Haven't I abused God's graces? Am I worthy of this mission? Will I have the courage I need? I've made so many resolutions, and I always fail."

There is always time to begin again and again.

We should not be discouraged if for half a lifetime we have not been fully faithful. If we only have five minutes left, it is for those five minutes that God has chosen us, for one last moment.

(Apostle and Apostolate, 47-49)

Lucien Cerfaux (1883-1968) was born in Belgium and studied for the priesthood in Rome. He served as professor of sacred scripture in the seminary of Tournai from 1911 to 1930, in which year he took over the chair of New Testament studies at the Catholic University of Louvain until his retirement in 1964. He served as a peritus at the Second Vatican Council and was a member of the Biblical Commission.

Fifteenth Sunday in Ordinary Time

Gospel: Luke 10:25-37

There was a lawyer who, to disconcert Jesus, stood up and said to him, "Master, what must I do to inherit eternal life?" Jesus said to him, "What is written in the law? What do you read there?"

Commentary: D. Bonhoeffer

And who is my neighbor? How often has this question been asked since, in good faith and genuine ignorance! It is plausible enough and any earnest seeker of the truth could reasonably ask it. But this is not the way the lawyer meant it. Jesus parries the question as a temptation of the devil, and that in fact is the whole point of the parable of the Good Samaritan. It is the sort of question you can keep on asking without ever getting an answer. Its source lies in the wrangling of men, corrupted in mind and bereft of truth; of men "doting about questions and disputes of words." From it come envy, strife, railings, even surmisings. It is the question of men who are puffed up, men who are "ever learning, and never able to come to knowledge of the truth." Of men "holding a form of godliness, but having denied the power thereof." They cannot believe, and they keep on asking this same question because they are *branded in their own conscience as with a hot iron*, because they refuse to obey the Word of God. *Who is my neighbor?* Does this question admit of any answer? Is it my kinsman, my compatriot, my brother Christian, or my enemy? There is an element of truth and falsehood in each of these answers. The whole question lands us into doubt and disobedience, and it is a veritable act of rebellion against the commandment of God. Of course, I say, I want to do his will, but he does not tell me how to set about it. The commandment does not give me any clear directions, and does nothing to solve my problems. The question *What shall I do?* was the lawyer's first attempt to throw dust in his own eyes. The answer was: "You know the commandments, do you not? Well, then, put them into practice. You must not ask questions — get on with the job!" And the final question *Who is my neighbor?* is the parting shot of despair (or else of self-confidence); the lawyer is trying to justify his disobedience. The answer is: "You are the neighbor. Go along and try to be obedient by loving others." Neighborliness is not a quality in other people, it is simply their claim on ourselves. Every moment and every situation challenges us to action and to obedience. We have literally no time to sit down and ask ourselves whether so-and-so is our neighbor or not. We must get into action and obey — we must behave like a neighbor to him. But perhaps this shocks you. Perhaps you still think you ought to think out beforehand and know what you ought to do. To that there is only one answer. You can only know and think about it by actually doing it. You can only learn what obedience is by obeying. It is no use asking questions; for it is only through obedience that you come to learn the truth.

With our consciences distracted by sin, we are confronted by the call of Jesus to spontaneous obedience. But whereas the rich young man was called to the grace of discipleship, the lawyer, who sought to tempt him, was only sent back to the commandment.

(The Cost of Discipleship, 66-68)

Dietrich Bonhoeffer (1906-1945), born in Breslau, Germany (then Silesia, Prussia), entered into ministry and studied at the University of Berlin. His thesis for his degree, *Communio Sanctorum*, became very famous then and now because it laid the foundation for all his writings. He studied also at Barcelona, Spain, and the Union Theological Seminary in New York. In 1931 he began teaching at the University of Berlin. In 1933 he was pastor of the German Lutheran congregation in London, but returned to Germany to join the resistance movement. Later he was arrested for his activities in the movement and imprisoned. He was hanged at thirty-nine years of age. While in prison he wrote some beautiful and lasting works. Bonhoeffer's thought has shaped the spirituality of the twentieth century.

Sixteenth Sunday in Ordinary Time

Gospel: Luke 10:38-42

Jesus came to a village, and a woman named Martha welcomed him into her house. She had a sister called Mary, who sat down at the Lord's feet and listened to him speaking.

Commentary: O. Prohászka

Martha, the busy woman, receives Jesus into her house, but even in his presence she is unable to stop work; she is so busy, there is so much to do! Whereas Mary is not working now; she sits at Jesus' feet and opens her soul to him. She has been working, and will work again later, but now she adores, loves, enjoys and is radiantly happy.

In Martha we are shown the imbalance of a life whose one urge is work and yet more work; a life that honors energy and perseverance but which neglects the inner world with its need to revivify the inmost depths of the soul, its care for spiritual beauty and freshness, of keeping one's intention pure and alert. There is something onesided here; Martha also should sit down in the Master's presence trying to enter into his soul. Time for work will be forthcoming afterwards. The main values are not what we produce by drive, talent, or hard work, but the motive behind all this — whether in our deepest self we are true to our supernatural principles, and strive to live up to them. Reality, self-awareness, ardent fidelity are the important things in life, and we have to devote time and constant unflagging interest to them.

When the obsession with work becomes unbalanced, it can make a person irritable, complaining, unjust to others. Work becomes a crushing yoke, a burden, instead of being a vocation gladly followed. Nowadays work is indeed a burden which weighs terribly upon humanity. Do not let us allow our soul to become embittered and deformed by work. Let us put our heart into our work, bring to it our goodwill and highest motives. This will be oil upon the grating wheels.

One thing is needed — a spirit united with God and living by him. With God for your life, your center, all your endeavors will be integrated as the circumference of this center. "Produce not more goods, but more happiness." The "one thing needful" is a pure, beautiful noble soul that loves God. Whoever chooses this has chosen the best part, and this is really the most logical procedure. Those who neglect the soul and themselves carry disunion within themselves; their fate is darkness, bitterness, and emptiness. But this does not mean that we should retire and hide in seclusion; let us remain at our post, but in all our work keep in mind *the one thing necessary*.

(*Meditations on the Gospels II*, 223-225)

Ottokar Prohászka (1858-1944), a native of Hungary, studied philosophy and theology at the Germanico-Hungaricum college at Rome, and was ordained in 1881. His powerful intellectual gifts were recognized at an early age, but he was no less concerned with the spiritual development of the seminarians in his charge and the pastoral care of the poor. From 1905 he lectured weekly at the University of Budapest on theology and science. Consecrated bishop that same year, he continued his spiritual, apostolic, and literary work simultaneously without intermission. Prohászka worked hard for social reform in Hungary and, having safely weathered the Communist Revolution, he was elected to the new Parliament in 1920. Vigorous and active until his death, Prohászka has been credited with having almost single-handedly brought about the reawakening of Hungarian spiritual culture.

Seventeenth Sunday in Ordinary Time

Gospel: Luke 11:1-13

Once Jesus was in a certain place praying, and when he had finished one of his disciples said, "Lord, teach us to pray, just as John taught his disciples."

Commentary: Teresa of Jesus

We can promise easily enough to give up our will to someone else, but when it comes to the test we find it the most difficult thing in the world to do perfectly. But God knows what each of us is able to bear, and when he finds a valiant soul he does not hesitate to accomplish his will in that person.

So I want to warn you and make you understand what God's will is, so that you may realize with whom you are dealing (as the saying goes) and what the good Jesus is offering on your behalf to the Father. I want to make sure you know what you are giving him when you say, "Your will be done." You are asking that God's will may be done in you; it is this and nothing else you are praying for. You need not be afraid he will give you wealth or pleasures or great honors or any earthly good things; his love for you is not so weak as that. He sets a far greater value on your gift and desires to reward you generously, giving you his kingdom even in this life. Would you like to see how he treats people who make this petition without reserve? Ask his glorious Son, who made it genuinely and resolutely in the garden. Was not God's will accomplished in him through the trials, the sufferings, the insults and the persecutions he sent him until at last his life was ended on the cross?

You see then what God gave to the one he loved best of all, and that shows you what his will is. These things are his gifts in this world, and he gives them in proportion to his love for us. To those he loves most he gives more, to those less dear he gives less; his gifts are measured by the courage he sees we have and the love we bear his Majesty. Fervent love can suffer a great deal for his sake, while lukewarmness will endure very little. I myself believe that love is the gauge of the crosses, great or small, that we are able to bear.

So if you have this love, think what you are doing. Do not let the promises you make to so great a Lord be no more than empty compliments, but brace yourselves to suffer whatever God wishes. Any other way of surrendering our will to him is like offering someone a precious stone, entreating him to accept it, and then holding on to it when he puts out his hand to take it. Such mockery is not for him who endured so much mockery for us. If for no other reason, it would be wrong to mock him in this way every time we say the Lord's Prayer. Let us give him once and for all the precious stone we have offered him so many times — for he in fact first gave us the thing we now give back to the Father.

My whole aim in writing this is to encourage us to yield ourselves entirely to our creator, to submit our will to his, and to detach ourselves from created things. Since you understand how important this is I will say no more on the subject, but will explain to you why our good Master wishes us to make this petition. He knows very well how we shall benefit by fulfilling the promise we have made to his eternal Father, for in a very short time we shall find ourselves at our journey's end, drinking at the fountain of living water.

(*Obras de Santa Teresa*, 238-242)

Teresa of Jesus (1515-1582) was born in Avila, Spain, and entered the Carmelites at eighteen years of age. She struggled with living the religious life, especially her prayer life, but grace finally won in 1555 when she resolved to give herself seriously to prayer and the life of perfection. She succeeded in inspiring the reform of the Carmelites with a vigorous apostolic spirit and in guiding her religious in the most lofty paths of prayer. Her writings were edited by her friend, Luis de León, O.S.A. In 1970 Pope Paul VI declared her a doctor of the Church.

Eighteenth Sunday in Ordinary Time

Gospel: Luke 12:13-21

A man in the crowd said to Jesus, "Master, tell my brother to give me a share of our inheritance."

Commentary: R. Guardini

Jesus tells the story of the wealthy landowner so wise in worldly wisdom, yet a fool in the eyes of God. "Take heed and guard yourselves from all covetousness, for a man's life does not consist in the abundance of his possessions." Here is the sharp division between the essential and the non-essential. Bread or life — which is the more important? Life, for when I am dead I no longer eat. Eternal possessions or temporal possessions — which are essential? Naturally the eternal ones, for the others fade away. What, therefore, should a man do? He should concentrate on the things of heaven, letting those of earth take their own course. His holdings should be in eternity, not in time. This is possible only through faith in Christ, which lifts the soul into life without end. Faith enables man to carry earthly existence over into immortality.

In the final analysis everything opposed to me and my Father is of no consequence. The more deeply people realize that Christ is the essential, the less concerned they will be about everything else. Thus they are armed for the struggle to come, given a foundation of eternal indestructibility: *Do not be afraid*. You will think yourself forsaken, but you will be safe and sound. Where? In the hands of divine providence. We have already seen what that means: not the order of nature, which exists in itself, but that order which exists between God and those who give themselves to him in true faith. To the extent that a man recognizes God as his Father, that he places his trust in him and makes his kingdom the primary concern of his heart, to precisely that extent a new order of being unfolds about him, one in which *For those who love God all things work together unto good*. And those who love God are those who hold fast to his Son. Tremendous word, condition for the realization of the providential order is Christ himself.

Jesus is attempting to anchor the hearts and minds of his disciples in reality. He wants them to sense what counts in God's eyes, and what does not; what he considers acceptable and what fallen. They are to complete the revaluation of existence that Jesus has begun. If they do this they will be prepared for anything. If the property they know to be "base wealth" (whatever its justification or cultural value) is taken from them because they love Christ, there is no loss. Needless to say, this is spoken to believers, and is effective only to the degree that their belief is active.

Thus Jesus roots his followers in the indestructible. Gently he immunizes them to all unreality: to the seeming authorities of the day to the world's wise and powerful and traditionally revered, to the prevailing social and economic order, to the dangers that threaten property, limb, and life. He is stripping them for the coming struggle, concentrating their forces, teaching them how to become invulnerable.

(*The Lord*, 179-182)

Romano Guardini (1885-1968), born at Verona in Italy, grew up in Mainz and was ordained in 1910. Ten years later he was admitted to the faculty of divinity at Bonn. In 1923 he became professor of dogmatic theology at Breslau and in 1945 professor of philosophy at Tübingen. His books were widely read by the laity and had great influence especially on the younger generation. They include: *The Lord, The Faith and Modern Man, The Living God*, and *Sacred Signs*.

Nineteenth Sunday in Ordinary Time

Gospel: Luke 12:32-48

Jesus said to his disciples: "See that you are dressed for action and have your lamps lit. Be like men waiting for their master to return from the wedding feast, ready to open the door as soon as he comes and knocks."

Commentary: K. Rahner

This world is a divided world. It is not merely a creation of God that has perhaps failed to achieve its full earthly perfection. This world in which culture, humanity, and the creative design of God are to be realized is also a world in which there is evil and darkness and hell. That is why man in all his creative activities, in all his earthly achievements and potentialities, in his literature and art and science and philosophy, is always liable to be seduced into falsity by the spirit of darkness, is always under the temptation to create a culture that is basically diabolical. That is why such a culture, such an earthly creation of man, must be exorcised and freed from all diabolical taint.

This is not entirely self-evident, as we know. We are in great danger of deceiving ourselves on this point. We tend to see the hand of the devil, the dark seductions of the abyss, only when we sin against the precepts of the book, against the express prohibitions of the ten commandments of God. And when we do not offend against them, then we think everything is in order, and we may easily find ourselves drifting with the tide, accepting as self-evident a "culture" that has been basically diabolized by the forces of debasement, by sheer luxury, by wild, senseless, formless, and unhallowed sexuality, by the demons of covetousness and pride and self-imprisonment in things of earth — all this can easily happen. We can let ourselves think that because a thing is obvious, because it is widespread, because everybody does it, it must be right and proper. We cannot let ourselves think that because this debased culture is widespread it must be acceptable, because it is widespread it must be right and even becoming for us. And if we fight against it, we can let ourselves think that we are fighting in the name of what we call the old values, and thus be merely preserving what was evil yesterday against what is evil and earthly and thoroughly worldly today. It is not as easy as all that for us Christians; we cannot fulfill our cultural mission by just saying yes and amen to every current trend, neither can we content ourselves with an appeal to the past, for that too must be subject to a judgment, to a discernment of spirits. So it is not as easy as all that for the Christian in his task, in his mission to this world, and to present-day life.

He must be a discerner of spirits. He must have the courage to say yes or no to both new and old alike, he must have the courage to develop by himself a Christian culture, a culture which belongs both to the present time and to God, a culture which is therefore a Christian, purified, and exorcised culture. This mission he can fulfill only with the help of courage and light and strength from above. Even so it will happen that this Christian leaven, when mixed with the dough of this world, is fated never to become entirely pure, entirely radiant, entirely aflame. We are still the laborers who must bear the heat and the burden of the day, who will never fully achieve the mission on which we are sent: for the fact remains that this culture, toward which we have a mission and a duty, which we are to perfect in a Christian manner, which we are to continually purify from the power of darkness and evil, will only reach its fulfillment in the kingdom of God. Before that comes about, we can, with the finger of God, show signs here and there that the kingdom of God has come into this world in the form of something bright and wholesome, something sound and true. More than this we cannot do. But even this is a noble mission set before us as men and as Christians, a mission against the darkness, to enkindle the faith that the kingdom of God is come.

(*Biblical Homilies*, 47-49)

Karl Rahner (1901-1984), a Swabian by birth, entered the Society of Jesus in 1922 and was ordained ten years later. After completing his studies at Freiburg and Innsbruck he was appointed to the theological faculty of Innsbruck in 1936. In 1949 he became a professor of dogmatic theology and in 1964 was appointed to a professorship in Munich. As a theological editor his name is associated with Denziger's *Enchiridion Symbolorum* and also with the *Lexicon für Theologie und Kirche* and *Sacramentum Mundi*. He was a peritus at Vatican II and the many volumes of *Theological Investigations* testify to his tireless labor as a theologian. Etienne Gilson drew attention to Rahner's "combination of intellectual modesty and audacity." A theologian of penetrating insight, he was also without doubt a man of God.

Twentieth Sunday
in Ordinary Time

Gospel: Luke 12:49-53

Jesus said to his disciples: "I have come to bring fire to the earth, and how I wish it were blazing already! There is a baptism I must still receive, and how great is my distress till it is over."

Commentary: J. Jeremias

Any attempt to sketch what Jesus expected in the future will have to start from his conviction that his mission was the prelude to the coming of the eschatological time of distress. Let no one imagine that he had come to bring peace — no, he brought a sword, fire on the earth, the cosmic baptism of suffering. Jesus was convinced that the suffering of his disciples was indissolubly linked with his own: he saw that his followers would be involved in a collective suffering, introduced by his passion. He was certain that the kingdom of God comes through suffering and only through suffering.

Jesus was convinced that his suffering would fundamentally alter the situation of his followers: the rejection of Jesus from Israel would also involve his disciples. Jesus' passion marks the turning point, the prelude to the time of the sword. To agree to follow Jesus means to venture on a life that is as hard as the last walk of a man condemned to death. For everyone, discipleship involves the readiness to tread the lonely road and to bear the people's hatred. For the disciples, the special sting of suffering will be the fulfillment of the words of the prophet Micah, *a man's enemies are the men of his own house*: the division will go right through the midst of families and the closest relatives; fathers, brothers, even a man's own children, will denounce them and deliver them up to death.

Jesus envisages martyrdom as the fate of his disciples. The law that the kingdom of God comes through suffering applies also to the disciples of Jesus. But suffering has the promise that the surrender of life is also the acceptance of life. God will deliver the one who endures to the end, who perseveres faithfully in the hour of trial, and prays to be delivered from the evil one. For this is Satan's work: he stands ready to sieve the disciples as a man sieves wheat.

Yet great as Satan's power is, God's power is greater. His victory is certain. When the temptation of the people of God reaches its climax, God will bring the great turning point. The little flock is promised that circumstances will be reversed. Despite its tiny number and the persecution that threatens, it may be sure that they are "the people of the saints of the Most High," to whom is promised "the kingdom and the dominion and the greatness of the kingdoms."

(New Testament Theology, 241-242)

Joachim Jeremias (1900-1979), born in Dresden, Germany, studied at the University of Leipzig. He taught in various universities in Germany. From 1935 onward he was professor of New Testament at the University of Göttingen, Germany. He is renowned in his field of the New Testament and has written numerous articles and books.

Twenty-First Sunday in Ordinary Time

Gospel: Luke 13:22-30

Through towns and villages Jesus went teaching, making his way to Jerusalem. Someone said to him: "Sir, will there be only a few saved?" Jesus said to them: "Try your best to enter by the narrow door, because, I tell you, many will try to enter and will not succeed."

Commentary: J. H. Newman

Nothing is more clearly brought out in Scripture, or more remarkable in itself than this, that in every age, out of the whole number of persons blessed with the means of grace, few only have duly availed themselves of this great benefit. So certain, so uniform is the fact, that it is almost stated as a doctrine. *Many are called, few are chosen.* Again, *Strive to enter in at the straight gate; for many, I say unto you, shall seek to enter in, and shall not be able.* And again, *Wide is the gate, and broad is the way, that leads to destruction, and many there by which go is thereat. Straight is the gate, and narrow is the way that leads unto life, and few there be that find it.*

The very temptation you lie under to explain away the plain words of Scripture shows you that your standard of good and evil, and the standard of all around you, must be very different from God's standard. It shows you, that if the chosen are few, there must be some particular belief necessary, or some particular line of conduct, or something else different from what the world supposes, in order to account for this solemn declaration. It suggests to you that perchance there must be a certain perfection, completeness, consistency, entireness of obedience, for a man to be chosen, which most men miss in one point or another. It suggests to you that there is a great difference between being a hearer of the word and a doer; a well-wisher of the truth. It suggests to you that it is one thing to be in earnest, another and higher to be *rooted and grounded in love*. It suggests to you the exceeding dangerousness of single sins, or particular bad habits. It suggests to you the peril of riches, cares of this life, station, and credit.

Of course we must not press the words of Scripture; we do not know the exact meaning of the word *chosen*; we do not know what is meant by being saved *so as by fire*; we do not know what is meant by *few*. But still the few can never mean the many; and to be called without being chosen cannot but be a misery. We know that the man in the parable who came to the feast without a wedding garment, was *cast into outer darkness*. Let us then set at nought the judgment of the many, whether about truth and falsehood, or about ourselves, and let us go by the judgment of that line of Saints, from the Apostles' times downwards, who were ever spoken against in their generation, ever honored afterwards — singular in each point of time as it came, but continuous and the same in the line of their history — ever protesting against the many, ever agreeing with each other. And, in proportion as we attain to their judgment of things, let us pray God to make it live in us; so that at the Last Day, when all veils are removed, we may be found among those who are inwardly what they seem outwardly — who with Enoch, and Noah, and Abraham, and Moses, and Joshua, and Caleb, and Phineas, and Samuel, and Elijah, and Jeremiah, and Ezekiel, and the Baptist, and Saint Paul, have *borne and had patience, and for his name-sake labored and not fainted*, watched in all things, done the work of an Evangelist, fought a good fight, finished their course, kept the faith.

(*Parochial and Plain Sermons*, volume 5, 254-255.267-269)

John Henry Newman (1801-1890) was born in London and brought up in the Church of England. He went up to Trinity College, Oxford, in 1817, became a Fellow of Oriel five years later, was ordained a deacon in 1824 and appointed vicar of Saint Mary's, Oxford, in 1832. The impact of his sermons was tremendous. He was the leading spirit in the Tractarian Movement (1833-1841) and the condemnation of "Tract 90" led to his resignation from Saint Mary's in 1843. Two years later he was received into the Catholic Church. He was ordained in Rome and founded a house of Oratorians in Birmingham. Newman's *Essay on the Development of Christian Doctrine* throws light on his withdrawal of previous objections to Roman Catholicism; his *Apologia* reveals the deepest motives underlying his outward attitudes, and *The Grammar of Assent* clarifies the subjective content of commitment to faith. In 1878 he was made a cardinal and he died at Edgbaston in 1890.

Twenty-Second Sunday in Ordinary Time

Gospel: Luke 14:1.7-14

On a sabbath Jesus had gone for a meal to the house of one of the leading Pharisees; and they watched him closely. He then told the guests a parable, because he had noticed how they picked the places of honor. He said this, "When someone invites you to a wedding feast, do not take your seat in the place of honor."

Commentary: Hildegard of Bingen

When you are invited to a wedding, do not take the first place, lest one more honorable than you should be invited, and he that invited you both should come and say to you, "Give this man your place"; and you with shame must go and take the last place. What does this mean? When you are told by divine inspiration that because of your faithful labors you are summoned to that holy tabernacle that flourishes in a bridal way of life, unceasingly rejoicing with purity and honor and holiness in the virginal branch and in the blessed Mother the Church, with no sadness or corruption or confusion or degradation of the bud or the flower, then curb your mind in humility and do not uplift it in pride. How?

When for love of God you free your body from earthly affairs, you will grow as a beautiful flower, blossoming and never withering in the heavenly Jerusalem with the Son of God, in whom are all ornaments for souls; for the old person produces all human abominations, but the new builds all the holiness of virtue. So when you have come to such holiness, blush to imitate the ancient serpent, who cast himself out of the place of beatitude because he was hungry for vainglory. What does this mean? If you see anyone better adorned than you, do not in eagerness of mind ascend above him, saying, "I want to be above him or like him!" If you exalt yourself so, are you a faithful servant, since you are provoking the

116

Lord to anger by opposing yourself to him? But if you see that someone has stronger resources than you, and out of envy disparage him, you are not walking on the plain road but going by trackless ways.

So be eager to serve God in humility and do not give yourself up madly to pride; and do not exalt yourself in vain pretense over one who, if assessed justly, shines with a greater desire of eternal life than you burn with yourself, and who for his heavenly ardor is invited to the height of blessedness by him who loves all lovers of truth. For if you do, he who by his inspiration summoned you to the service of humility and the other to the gift of charity may come with the eye of knowledge and judge you with his righteous judgment, saying, "You lifted yourself up in eager pride to a place for which you are not fit; leave your vainglory and submit in duty, and give this beloved one of mine the place of honor you so rashly seized!" And what will become of you then?

If you are overthrown in this way, in anguish of grief and sadness you will begin to feel extreme defection and abhor yourself as contemptible; for the Protector of souls will take you the honor you usurped when you opposed yourself to him and tried to seize what was not yours to have. So what you wanted will be taken from you, and what you did not want will be given to you. And so also when a lesser order exalts itself over a greater one it will be suppressed, overthrown by my just judgment, for I do not wish that pride to be anything but thrown down and confounded. For if a handmaid exalts herself above her mistress, she will be despised the more by all who see her, for she tried to become what she should not have desired.

(*Scivias*, 219-220)

Hildegard of Bingen (1098-1179), was a German nun, mystic, and scholar. Having entered religious life as a child, Hildegard founded the Benedictine convent of Rupertberg near Bingen in 1147. Renowned for her visions, related in the *Scivias*, Hildegard was a theologian, physician, and composer as well as an energetic reformer.

Twenty-Third Sunday in Ordinary Time

Gospel: Luke 14:25-33

Great crowds accompanied Jesus on his way and he turned and spoke to them. "If any man comes to me without hating his father, mother, wife, children, brothers, sisters, yes and his own life too, he cannot be my disciple."

Commentary: A. de Mello

What is happiness? Very few people know and no one can tell you, because happiness cannot be described. Can you describe light to people who have been sitting in darkness all their lives? Can you describe reality to someone in a dream? Understand your darkness and it will vanish; then you will know what light is. Understand your nightmare for what it is and it will stop; then you will wake up to reality. Understand your false beliefs and they will drop; then you will know the taste of happiness.

If people want happiness so badly, why don't they attempt to understand their false beliefs? First, because it never occurs to them to see them as false or even as beliefs. They see them as facts and reality, so deeply have they been programmed. Second, because they are scared to lose the only world they know: the world of desires, attachments, fears, social pressures, tensions, ambitions, worries, guilt, with flashes of the pleasure of relief and excitement which these things bring. Think of someone who is afraid to let go of a nightmare because, after all, that is the only world he knows. There you have a picture of yourself and of other people.

If you wish to attain to lasting happiness you must be ready to hate father, mother, even your own life and to take leave of all your possessions. How? Not by renouncing them or giving them up because what you give up violently you are forever bound to. But rather by seeing them for the nightmare they are; and then,

118

whether you keep them or not, they will have lost their grip over you, their power to hurt you, and you will be out of your dream at last, out of your darkness, your fear, your unhappiness.

So spend some time seeing each of the things you cling to for what it really is, a nightmare that causes you excitement and pleasure on the one hand but also worry, insecurity, tension, anxiety, fear, unhappiness on the other.

Father and mother: nightmare. Wife and children, brothers and sisters: nightmare. All your possessions: nightmare. Your life as it is now: nightmare. Every single thing you cling to and have convinced yourself you cannot be happy without: nightmare. Then you will hate father and mother, wife and children, brothers and sisters and even your own life. And you will so easily take leave of all your possessions, that is, you will stop clinging and thus have destroyed their capacity to hurt you. Then at last you will experience that mysterious state that cannot be described or uttered — the state of abiding happiness and peace. And you will understand how true it is that everyone who stops clinging to brothers and sisters, father, mother or children, land or houses . . . is repaid a hundred times over and gains eternal life.

(The Way to Love, 7-9)

Anthony de Mello was a Jesuit priest and the director of the Sadhana Institute of Pastoral Counseling in Poona, India. He is the author of *Sadhana, The Song of the Bird, The Heart of the Enlightened, Taking Flight, Wellsprings,* and *Awareness. The Way to Love* is a never-before-published collection of the last meditations written by Anthony de Mello before his untimely death in 1987.

Twenty-Fourth Sunday in Ordinary Time

Gospel: Luke 15:1-32

The tax collectors and the sinners were all seeking the company of Jesus to hear what he had to say, and the Pharisees and the scribes complained. "This man," they said, "welcomes sinners and eats with them." So he spoke this parable to them: "What man among you with a hundred sheep, losing one, would not leave the ninety-nine in the wilderness and go after the missing one till he found it?"

Commentary: Juan of Avila

*L*ord, you came looking for the lost sheep and you placed it on your shoulders." — I had to explain to you how the Son of God came on his quest, leaving behind his royal palace and its table and his Father's music. He desired to come to where the lost sheep was and to don its garments and accept its toils.

Have you ever seen a starry sky as beautiful as the sight of Jesus Christ coming with the little sheep in his arms? — "Look, Lord, if the little sheep is a bit rebellious, you won't strike it, will you? And if it asks you, Lord, to put it down, you still will not put it down, will you?"

O blessed shoulders of Jesus Christ! What is to be said of these shoulders? What does it mean to say that he takes the little sheep on his shoulders? It means that Jesus Christ washes the feet of his disciples and kisses them and says: "My disciples, do you understand what I have done? Don't you grasp what I mean you to realize when I do this? I want you to realize that if I, your Lord and Master, wash your feet, you are also to wash one another's feet." Then Jesus Christ says: "Do you see me coming with the little sheep on my shoulders? I am trying to tell you that you are to bear one another's burdens and toils and difficulties. And not

120

as some do who seem to have shoulders made of pastry dough, for if they are told they have to be peacemakers, they answer: Who is trying to involve me in other people's quarrels?"

To travel on the shoulders of Jesus Christ means that on his shoulders your fasting, almsgiving, and prayers have value, precisely because you are on Christ's shoulders and supported by his merits, apart from which your words are worthless. Get up on his shoulders, therefore, because he has won us all by carrying our sins on his cross and on his shoulders. *Authority and government are on his shoulders.* He won his kingdom by carrying the cross on his shoulders; get up, therefore, on his shoulders, because while he is carrying you, God will not wreak vengeance on you.

And if people say that they can leave it to the Lord to punish his servants, Christ will say to the Lord: "Lord, if you will not forgive them because they are my servants, consider that they are my brothers and sisters and brides, and if this is not enough, consider that they are my members and indeed are one with me. And if it is not possible to punish the members without punishing the head as well, but quite the contrary, then their being members of my body is reason enough. *For no one hates his own flesh.*" All the more, then, is their being members of Jesus Christ reason enough to love and help them. If you saw Jesus Christ himself and received him into your home and gave him what he needed, this would not be deserving of great praise. Any wicked man or woman, knowing it to be Christ, would do the same. But if you receive the poor because they belong to him and because he commands it, this is a sign of greater love. And just as he took us on his shoulders, so let us take our brothers and sisters on our shoulders, and let us not have wax shoulders that cannot support even an ounce of weight.

(*Sermones*, Ciclo temporal, Dom. 3 después de Pentecostés, 306-307)

Juan of Avila (1499-1569), born in Almodovan del Campo in Spain, for thirty years criss-crossed Spain preaching the gospel and winning many people to embrace the faith. He also began a missionary society, founded schools, wrote commentaries on scripture, and engaged in much correspondence with different people. All this he did in spite of failing health.

Twenty-Fifth Sunday in Ordinary Time

Gospel: Luke 16:1-13

Jesus said to his disciples, "There was a rich man and he had a steward who was denounced to him for being wasteful with his property."

Commentary: K. Rahner

Our life is a series of vicissitudes. The landscape of the soul is exposed to every kind of weather. By turns we are happy and unhappy; now lively, now weary; now pleased with our surroundings, now disappointed and hurt; now young, now old; now encouraged by success, now crushed by some bitter failure; now grateful for all the benefits we receive, now wounded by the thought of all that is denied us. Ups and downs, like those of the steward in the gospel. But are we as prudent as he was? Have we the faith, the stout heart, the humble mind, the docility to God's good pleasure, to see in the most contrasting fortunes of our lives a chance to bring forth fruit for eternity, to prove our love for God, to be patient and courageous, unassuming and devoted; or do we insist on having our own way in the service that we offer God, are we prepared to find him only in the particular situation we have chosen? Before we know it, he has sent us a different situation; and we have not the magnanimity, the willing, loving, uninhibited prudence, to perceive God's call, his work for us, in the different situation, to accept it with a will, to get on with it, to be well-content with God's good pleasure for us. We are not so prudent as the steward in the gospel. And yet we should be. If the heart is really kept open and ready for God, anything that may happen to us in life can be accepted as a grace and a blessing. Of course this means having a heart that is well disposed and humble, that listens and obeys. But why not ask God for that gift? Could we not pray instead of complaining, call on God instead of accusing others? Somewhere in the life of every human being is a wound that has never healed. For we should be saints in the literal sense of the word — holy people — if always and in all things we were at one with God and his will. It is because we are not that the parable of the Christian's heavenly prudence concerns us all. If we will only look a little more closely at our lives, we shall find situations, relationships, burdens, here and there, that can only be seen for what they are, can only be coped with, if we are prudent enough by God's grace to acknowledge with a heavenly prudence: This too is a word of God's eternal love; I must be loving and courageous and answer yes.

(Biblical Homilies, 59-61)

Karl Rahner (1901-1984), a Swabian by birth, entered the Society of Jesus in 1922 and was ordained ten years later. After completing his studies at Freiburg and Innsbruck he was appointed to the theological faculty of Innsbruck in 1936. In 1949 he became a professor of dogmatic theology and in 1964 was appointed to a professorship in Munich. As a theological editor his name is associated with Denziger's *Enchiridion Symbolorum* and also with the *Lexicon für Theologie und Kirche* and *Sacramentum Mundi*. He was a peritus at Vatican II and the many volumes of *Theological Investigations* testify to his tireless labor as a theologian. Etienne Gilson drew attention to Rahner's "combination of intellectual modesty and audacity." A theologian of penetrating insight, he was also without doubt a man of God.

Twenty-Sixth Sunday in Ordinary Time

Gospel: Luke 16:19-31

Jesus said to the Pharisees: "There was a rich man who used to dress in purple and fine linen and feast magnificently every day. At his gate there lay a poor man called Lazarus, covered with sores."

Commentary: H. Thielicke

The mercy of God is boundless, yes, but it is not offered indefinitely. Here we are still living by the grace of God and the merit of Christ; the sentence is still punctuated with a colon. We still have a reprieve, a season of grace; we still have time to live and turn back home. But one day comes — finality, period.

And then even Lazarus will not be able to come to us, and Father Abraham will not be able to send him to add one extenuating phrase or happy ending to this full stop. Lazarus once waited for the crumb of bread from the rich man's table; now the rich man waits for the drop at the end of Lazarus' finger. But the hour of visitation, the hour of the waiting, expectant mercy of God has run out. The "acceptable time," the *kairos*, is past. Now there is only the yawning chasm that none can pass over.

And here in the extremity of his need the rich man feels, for the first time, something like love. Of all places he feels it in hell, where at best he may feel it but can no longer exercise it, where it lies dammed up within him, incapable of expression and causing him only further torment. He is thinking of his five brothers and with horror he sees them going on living their lives, in innocence, stumbling along without the slightest notion that in this life nothing less than our eternal destiny is at stake. What a torment it is to be forced to think of them as the rich man is compelled to think of them and see them here in hell! It is the torment of the dead that they cannot warn the living, just as it is the torment of the mature that the erring young will not listen to them.

You are one of the five brothers of the rich man — that's the focal point in this message. *You* are the one — you, who may perhaps be sauntering down the broad road of your life, still young and with so much of the future before you; you, who, it may be, considers the mysterious goal of this road to be no more than a figment of religious fancy and the crossroads where you now stand just any arbitrary point on the way.

Do not imagine that a messenger will come from the beyond and confirm what is said in Moses and the prophets, what seems to you to be so unverifiable, so mythological. Father Abraham will *not* send you any such occult confirmation. For anybody who has an interest in evading God will also consider an appearance from the dead an empty specter and delusion. Nor will the heavens open above us and God will perform no miracle to bring us to our knees. For God is no shock therapist who works upon our nerves; he loves you as his child and it's your heart he wants.

So there will be no one appearing from the dead, no voice from heaven will sound, nor will there be any miracle in the clouds. *None* of this will come to you — you, who are one of the rich man's five brothers. We have only the Word, the Word made flesh and crucified, that namelessly quiet Word which came to us in one who was as poor and despised as his brother Lazarus. For he really wanted to be his brother. And that's why there could be no brass bands to march before him. That's why he renounced all royal pomp and show. That's why he had to risk the effect of ambiguity and forgo the demonstration of his power.

He wanted to be the brother of the poorest and in *this* way show them his love.

(*The Waiting Father, The Parables of Jesus*, 48-50)

Helmut Thielicke (1908-1986), born in Wüppertel-Bermen, Germany, earned doctorate degrees in philosophy and theology from the University of Erlanger. He taught at the University of Heidelberg and then was ordained a priest in 1941 in the Lutheran Church. From 1943 to 1954 he was professor of systematic theology at the University of Tübingen, Germany, and then rector of the University. In 1951 he then became professor of systematic theology at the University of Hamburg and became rector in 1960. He authored numerous books and articles.

Twenty-Seventh Sunday in Ordinary Time

Gospel: Luke 17:5-10

The apostles said to the Lord: "Increase our faith." The Lord replied, "Were your faith the size of a mustard seed you could say to this mulberry tree, 'Be uprooted and planted in the sea,' and it would obey you."

Commentary: G. Bornkamm

Jesus promises to those who do God's will God's reward in the kingdom of heaven. Innumerable sayings and parables contain this idea of reward: its concern is man's position before God. God is Lord and man his servant. Strictly speaking, however, man's relationship to God as that of a servant certainly excludes the thought of reward, or at least limits it. For the servant is the master's own property, his slave whose body and life belong to him, and who has no special claim on reward. Hence the saying: "We are unworthy servants, we have only done what was our duty." The master is entitled to claim his servant completely. As far as the servant is concerned, however, the work he has been given is not his own, the services which he is obliged to render do not rest with him. He is therefore required to be faithful, faithful in the face of his master's strange, superior will. Hence in a strict sense the idea of reward has nothing at all to do with the relationship between master and slave, for the latter has no property, but is his master's property.

The reward which is nevertheless promised in Jesus' parables to the disciples as servants is not a payment which is owed, but a mark of distinction with which the trusted servant is rewarded as a sign of even greater trust. This is shown in the parables of the servants who want for their Lord, as in that of the talents. *I will set you over much. Enter into the joy of your Master!* Here the servant is not paid and dismissed, but is received into the closest and most lasting fellowship with his master.

126

Before God, the wise and faithful servant is one who is faithful to his task, faithful in the management and increase of the estate entrusted to him, faithful in his love toward the least of Jesus' disciples, and constantly ready for action, with his torch alight. His waiting is not for the nothingness of the unknown, not for the silence of death, but for the Lord who has met and will meet his disciples, the Lord who *will gird himself, and have them sit at table, and himself come and serve them.*

(*Jesus of Nazareth*, 137-138)

Günther Bornkamm (1905-   ), born in Görtitz, Germany, taught at the University of Konigsburg. With World War II he became a minister in Bethel, Germany. After the war he resumed teaching theology at the University of Heidelberg where he also served as dean of the faculty of theology and rector of the university. He is the author of several books.

Twenty-Eighth Sunday in Ordinary Time

Gospel: Luke 17:11-19

On the way to Jerusalem Jesus traveled along the border between Samaria and Galilee. As he entered one of the villages, ten lepers came to meet him. They stood some way off and called to him, "Jesus! Master! Take pity on us." When he saw them, he said, "Go and show yourselves to the priests."

Commentary: M. Luther

In the leper the gospel teaches us faith, in Christ it teaches us love. Now, as I have often said, faith and love constitute the whole character of the Christian. Faith receives, love gives. Faith brings man to God, love brings man to his fellow. Through faith he permits God to do him good, through love he does good to his brother man. For whoever believes has every thing from God, and is happy and rich. Therefore he needs henceforth nothing more, but all he lives and does, he orders for the good and benefit of his neighbor, and through love he does to his neighbor as God did to him through faith. Thus he reaps good from above through faith, and gives good below through love. Against this kind of life, work righteous persons with their merits and good works terribly contend for they do works only to serve themselves, they live only unto themselves, and do good without faith. These two principles, faith and love, we will now consider as they appear in the lepers and in Christ.

In the first place it is a characteristic of faith to presume to trust God's grace, and it forms a bright vision and refuge in God, doubting nothing; it thinks God will have regard for his faith, and not forsake it. For where there is no such vision and confidence, there is no true faith, and there is also no true prayer nor any seeking after God. But where it exists it makes man bold and anxious, freely to bring his troubles unto God, and earnestly to pray for help.

Observe here in the leper how faith is constituted, how without any teacher at all it teaches us how our prayers may be truly fruitful. You here observe how they had a good opinion of and a comforting assurance in Christ, and firmly thought he would be gracious to them.

The lepers have instructed us how to believe; Christ teaches us to love. Love does to our neighbor as it sees Christ has done to us, as he says in John 13:15: *For I have given you an example, that you also should do as I have done to you.* And immediately afterward he says in verse 34: *A new commandment I give unto you, that you love one another.* What else does this mean than to say: Through me in faith you now have everything that I am and have: I am your own, you are now rich and satisfied through me; for all I do and love I do and love not for my but only for your sake, and I only think how to be useful and helpful to you, and accomplish whatever you need and should have. Therefore consider this example, to do to each other as I have done to you, and only consider how to be useful to your neighbor, and do what is useful and necessary for him. Your faith has enough in my love and grace; so your love shall also give enough to others.

Behold, this is a Christian life, and in brief it does not need much doctrine nor many books; it is wholly contained in faith and love.

(Sermons, 63-64.69-70)

Martin Luther (1483-1546), born in Eisleben, Germany, was preparing for a vocation in law when, in the summer of 1505, he was caught in a violent thunderstorm and knocked to the ground by a bolt of lightning. This experience seemed to provide a culmination and partial answer to the religious questions that troubled him, and two weeks later he entered the Augustinian monastery at Erfurt. In 1508 he became professor of theology at the University of Wittenberg; and in 1517, to protest the corrupt sale of indulgences by the Church, he nailed ninety-five theses challenging this practice to the door of the Castle Church in Wittenberg. This proved to be the spark that ignited the Protestant Reformation.

Twenty-Ninth Sunday in Ordinary Time

Gospel: Luke 18:1-8

Jesus told his disciples a parable about the need to pray continually and never lose heart. "There was a judge in a certain town," he said, "who had neither fear of God nor respect for man. In the same town there was a widow who kept on coming to him and saying, 'I want justice from you against my enemy.'"

Commentary: F. Faber

If people have ever indulged in judging others, the mere sight of an action almost involuntarily suggests an internal commentary upon it. It has become so natural to judge, however little their own duties or responsibilities are connected with what they are judging, that the actions of others present themselves to the mind as in the attitude of asking a verdict from it. All our fellow-human beings who come within the reach of our knowledge, and for the most retired of us the circle is a wide one, are prisoners at the bar; and if we are unjust, ignorant, capricious judges, it must be granted to us that we are indefatigable ones.

Now all this is simple ruin to our souls. At any risk, at the cost of life, there must be an end of this, or it will end in everlasting banishment from God. The standard of the last judgment is absolute. It is this the measure which we have meted to others. Our present humor in judging others reveals to us what our sentence would be if we died now. Are we content to abide that issue? But, as it is impossible all at once to stop judging, and as it is also impossible to go on judging uncharitably, we must pass through the intermediate stage of kind interpretations. Few have passed beyond this to a habit of perfect charity, which has blessedly stripped them of their judicial ermine and their deeply rooted judicial habits of mind. We ought, therefore, to cultivate most sedulously the habit of kind interpretations.

People's actions are very difficult to judge. Their real character depends in a great measure on the motives which prompt them, and those motives are invisible to us. Appearances are often against what we afterwards discover to have been deeds of virtue. Moreover, a line of conduct is, in its look at least, very little like a logical process. It is complicated with all manner of inconsistencies, and often deformed by what is in reality a hidden consistency. Nobody can judge men and women but God, and we can hardly obtain a higher or more reverent view of God than that which represents him to us as judging them with perfect knowledge, unperplexed certainty, and undisturbed compassion. Now, kind interpretations are imitations of the merciful ingenuity of the Creator finding excuses for his creatures. It is almost a day of revelation to us when theology enables us to perceive that God is so merciful precisely because he is so wise; and from this truth it is an easy inference that kindness is our best wisdom, because it is an image of the wisdom of God.

(*Kindness*, 54-57)

Frederick Faber (1814-1863) was born at Calverley, Yorkshire, and studied at Oxford, where he won the Newdigate prize for poetry in 1836. Under Newman's influence he became a Catholic in 1845, with many of his friends. He was ordained a priest in 1847, and placed himself under Newman as a novice at the Birmingham Oratory. In 1849 he was sent to found an Oratory in London, which later became the Brompton oratory. Here he became widely known for his preaching, hymns and devotional writings, which appealed to both the emotions and the intellect. His books were translated into many European languages.

Thirtieth Sunday
in Ordinary Time

Gospel: Luke 18:9-14

Jesus spoke the following parable to some people who prided themselves on being virtuous and despised everyone else: "Two men went up to the temple to pray, one a Pharisee, the other a tax collector."

Commentary: M. Luther

You have in the publican a beautiful example of true Christian repentance and faith, and an excellent masterpiece of high spiritual wisdom or theology, of which the Pharisee and those like him have never received a taste or smell. Besides you see here the proper fruits that follow faith, that he is now a different man, with a different mind, thoughts, words, and works than formerly; he gives honor and praise to God alone for his divine grace; he calls and prays to him from the heart and in true confidence in his Word and promise; otherwise he could not have either thought or prayed these words; and thus he performs unto God the true and acceptable worship, and observes the true Sabbath. And now he also has a heart which is an enemy to sin and disobedience. He does not rejoice but is sorry that he has lived in violation of God's commandments, and now he earnestly and from his whole heart seeks to forsake his evil ways, not to offend, deceive, belie, nor treat anyone unjustly or with violence, and anxiously desires that even thus everyone should live in the same way.

This is the picture of today's gospel, of the two kinds of persons among those called God's people. One kind is the great faction of the false church, who nevertheless bear the appearance and the name as though they alone were the most pious and sanctified servants of God; the other, the little flock of those who are true members of the church and true children of God, although they have not praise and great reputation before the world. The difference between them is that each party is known by its characteristics and fruits, by which the appearance and name should be distinguished from their true nature, of which you have sufficiently heard.

Therefore see to it that you properly follow this publican and become like him. Namely, in the first place, that you be not a false but a real sinner; not only in words but in reality and from the heart acknowledge yourself worthy before God and his wrath and eternal punishment, and bring before him in truth these words, "me a poor sinner"; but in the same flight lay hold of the other words: *Be merciful to me,* by which words you take away the point and edge of the law and thus cast and turn from you the judgment and condemnation the law seeks to force upon you.

From this distinction in the two kinds of sinners you are able to form a correct estimate of both sides.

(Sermons, 366-367)

Martin Luther (1483-1546), born in Eisleben, Germany, was preparing for a vocation in law when, in the summer of 1505, he was caught in a violent thunderstorm and knocked to the ground by a bolt of lightning. This experience seemed to provide a culmination and partial answer to the religious questions that troubled him, and two weeks later he entered the Augustinian monastery at Erfurt. In 1508 he became professor of theology at the University of Wittenberg; and in 1517, to protest the corrupt sale of indulgences by the Church, he nailed ninety-five theses challenging this practice to the door of the Castle Church in Wittenberg. This proved to be the spark that ignited the Protestant Reformation.

Thirty-First Sunday in Ordinary Time

Gospel: Luke 19:1-10

Jesus entered Jericho and was going through a town when a man whose name was Zacchaeus made his appearance; he was one of the senior tax collectors and a wealthy man. He was anxious to see what kind of man Jesus was, but he was too short and could not see him for the crowd.

Commentary: Elizabeth of the Trinity

*I*n order to understand this very mysterious saying *Remain in me*, we must not, so to speak, stop at the surface, but enter ever deeper into the divine Being through recollection. *I pursue my course*, exclaimed Saint Paul; so must we descend daily this pathway of the abyss which is God; let us slide down this slope in wholly loving confidence. *Deep calls unto deep.* It is there in the very depths that the divine impact takes place, where the abyss of our nothingness encounters the abyss of mercy, the immensity of the all of God. There we will find the strength to die to ourselves and, losing all vestige of self, we will be changed into love. . . . "Blessed are those who die in the Lord!"

The kingdom of God is within you. A while ago God invited us to "remain in him," to live spiritually in his glorious heritage, and now he reveals to us that we do not have to go out of ourselves to find him: *The kingdom of God is within!* Saint John of the Cross says that "it is in the substance of the soul where neither the devil nor the world can reach" that God gives himself to it; then "all its movements are divine, and although they are from God they also belong to the soul, because God works them in it and with it."

The same saint also says that "God is the center of the soul. So when the soul with all" its "strength will know God perfectly, love and enjoy him fully, then it will have reached the deepest center that can be attained in him." Before attaining this, the soul is

134

already "in God who is its center," but it is not yet in its *deepest* center, for it can still go further. Since love is what unites to God, the more intense this love is, the more deeply the soul enters into God and the more it is centered in him. When it "possesses even one degree of love it is already in its center"; but when this love has attained its perfection, the soul will have penetrated into its *deepest* center. There it will be transformed to the point of becoming very like God. To this soul living within can be addressed the words of Père Lacordaire to Saint Mary Magdalene: "No longer ask for the Master among those on earth or in heaven, for he is your soul and your soul is he."

Hurry and come down, for I must stay in your house today. The Master unceasingly repeats this word to our soul which he once addressed to Zacchaeus. *Hurry and come down.* But what is this descent that he demands of us except an entering more deeply into our interior abyss? This act is not "an external separation from external things," but a "solitude of spirit," a detachment from all that is not God.

"As long as our will has fancies that are foreign to divine union, whims that are now yes, now no, we are like children; we do not advance with giant steps in love for fire has not yet burnt up all the alloy; the gold is not pure; we are still seeking ourselves; God has not consumed" all our hostility to him. But when the boiling cauldron has consumed "every imperfect love, every imperfect sorrow, every imperfect fear," "then love is perfect and the golden ring of our alliance is larger than heaven and earth. This is the secret cellar in which love places his elect," this "love leads us by ways and paths known to him alone; and he leads us with no turning back, for we will not retrace our steps."

(*Conferences*, 94-96)

Elizabeth of the Trinity (1880-1906), a Carmelite nun born Elizabeth Catez near Boureges, France, was influenced by John of the Cross, Thérèse of Lisieux, and Jan van Ruysbroeck. Her spirituality, which leads through deepening silence to the indwelling Trinity, is strongly Christocentric. She sees transformation into the image of God taking place on earth as individuals relive the mysteries of the Incarnate Word in their personal humanity. In the Letter of Paul to the Ephesians, she found her "new name," Praise of Glory (1:12). Her writings emphasize heaven and eternity permeating every temporal moment. She died in 1906 of Addison's disease.

Thirty-Second Sunday in Ordinary Time

Gospel: Luke 20:27-38

Some Sadducees — those who say that there is no resurrection — approached Jesus and they put this question to him, "Master, we have it from Moses in writing, that if a man's married brother dies childless, the man must marry the widow to raise up children for his brother."

Commentary: J. H. Newman

God spoke to Moses in the burning bush, and called himself the *God of Abraham*; and Christ tells us that in this simple announcement was contained the promise that Abraham should rise again from the dead. In truth, if we may say it with reverence, the All-wise, All-knowing God cannot speak without meaning many things at once. He sees the end from the beginning; he understands the numberless connections and relations of all things one with another. Look at Christ's words, and this same character of them will strike you; whatever he says is fruitful in meaning, and refers to many things. It is well to keep this in mind when we read scripture.

When God called himself the God of Abraham, Isaac, and Jacob, he implied that those holy patriarchs were still alive, though they were no more seen on earth. This may seem evident at first sight; but it may be asked how the text proves that their *bodies* would live; for, if their *souls* were still living, that would be enough to account for their being still called in the Book of Exodus servants of God. Our blessed Lord seems to tell us, that in some sense or other Abraham's *body* might be considered still alive as a pledge of his resurrection, though it was dead in the common sense in which we apply the word. His announcement is, Abraham *shall* rise from the dead, because in truth he *is* still alive. He cannot in the end be held under the power of the grave, any more than a sleeping man can be kept from waking. Abraham is still alive in the dust, though not risen thence. He is alive because all God's saints live to him, though they seem to perish.

We are apt to talk about our bodies as if we knew how or what they really were; whereas we only know what our eyes tell us. They seem to grow, to come to maturity, to decay; but after all we know no more about them then meets our senses. We have no direct cognizance of what may be called the substantive existence of the body, only of its accidents. Again, we are apt to speak of *soul and body*, as if we could distinguish between them, and knew much about them; but for the most part we use words without meaning. It is useful to make the distinction, and Scripture makes it; but after all the gospel speaks of our nature, in a religious sense, *as one*. Soul and body make up one man, which is born once and never dies. Philosophers of old time thought the soul indeed might live forever, but that the body perished at death; but Christ tells us otherwise. He tells us the body will live forever. In the text he seems to intimate that it never really dies; that we lose sight indeed of what *we* are accustomed to see, but that God still sees the elements of it which are not exposed to our senses.

God graciously called himself *the God of Abraham*. He did not say the God of Abraham's soul, but simply of "Abraham." He blest Abraham, and he gave him eternal life; not to his soul only, without his body, but to Abraham as one man.

(*Parochial and Plain Sermons*, volume 1, 271-273)

John Henry Newman (1801-1890) was born in London and brought up in the Church of England. He went up to Trinity College, Oxford, in 1817, became a Fellow of Oriel five years later, was ordained a deacon in 1824 and appointed vicar of Saint Mary's, Oxford, in 1832. The impact of his sermons was tremendous. He was the leading spirit in the Tractarian Movement (1833-1841) and the condemnation of "Tract 90" led to his resignation from Saint Mary's in 1843. Two years later he was received into the Catholic Church. He was ordained in Rome and founded a house of Oratorians in Birmingham. Newman's *Essay on the Development of Christian Doctrine* throws light on his withdrawal or previous objections to Roman Catholicism; his *Apologia* reveals the deepest motives underlying his outward attitudes, and *The Grammar of Assent* clarifies the subjective content of commitment to faith. In 1879 he was made a cardinal and he died at Edgbaston in 1890.

Thirty-Third Sunday in Ordinary Time

Gospel: Luke 21:5-19

When some were talking about the temple, remarking how it was adorned with fine stonework and votive offerings, Jesus said, "All these things you are staring at now — the time will come when not a single stone will be left on another; everything will be destroyed."

Commentary: J. Moltmann

Two things concern all of us daily: first, the future of God, for we believe in hope and expect the fulfillment of all our prayers. But at the same time also, we are concerned about the future of the earth on which we live and work, love and suffer with others. We recognize the coming famine, and we would like to have peace and righteousness on earth so that our children can be happy, so that they will live with the children of all other people in a human way. We read the Bible and we read the newspaper every day. As we read the Bible, we would like to participate in the promised history of God. As we read the newspaper, we would like to be involved in the fate of the world. But how can we bring both together: community with hope in God and community with the sorrows of the earth?

But whoever perseveres in hope remains in love. Because we hope in Christ, we do not let ourselves be embittered by all disappointments. We persevere in the love of Christ for the degraded and the wronged. We bring friendliness into a world of cold indifference. We are "fools" of love because we always give an advance of trust.

And then there is the other: *"This gospel of the kingdom will be preached throughout the whole world, as a testimony to all nations; and then the end will come."* Perseverance until the end; that means going on ahead with the message of freedom and of the kingdom, penetrating to all places and circumstances with the conviction that the end is the kingdom of Christ. The only person who will remain until the end will be the one who, on God's account, does not stay where he is but goes on ahead; who goes to meet the coming God in the world. Christians do not have a point of view to defend, but a way they must travel and a front on which to battle the real suffering in the world that exists right now. At this front we should ignite with the gospel hope in an open, outgoing life and awaken faith in the haughty and the despised. On this front of sorrowing and oppressed creatures we must disseminate friendliness and love through their solidarity.

And — then the end of the world need!

That is the last thing. Notice that it does not precede the descriptions of wars, catastrophes, and famines. It simply means that those things are not yet the end. Christian hope is no frightful expectation of catastrophes. Christ is not coming as "the great destroyer of all things" (Christoph Blumhardt), but here, where, in the dark history of hunger and war and earthquake, friendliness is disseminated, where the gospel of the kingdom is brought to all people for the witness of their hope. Here for the first time it is certain and definitive: "And then the end will come."

Christian hope is thus the hope of the love which takes the sorrow of humanity upon itself and looks for the kingdom where "peace and joy laugh." And Christ is coming as the judge who comforts all the deeply afflicted and raises the suffering to freedom.

(*The Gospel of Liberation*, 111-112)

Jürgen Moltmann (1926-), born in Hamburg, Germany, received his doctorate in theology from the University of Göttingen. He was pastor of the evangelical church in Bremen, Germany, and then professor of theology at the University of Bonn, 1963-1967, and from 1967 professor at the University of Tübingen, Germany. He authored books and articles on various themes.

Christ the King

Gospel: Luke 23:35-43

The people stayed there watching Jesus. As for the leaders, they jeered at him. "He saved others," they said; "let him save himself if he is the Christ of God, the Chosen One."

Commentary: S. Schneiders

The true royalty of Jesus, which had nothing to do with the royal consciousness, but was rooted in his divine filiation, was expressed in his identification with the reign of God. Consequently, it was not something he could claim during his public life because he knew well that the royal consciousness was as much at work in the hearts of the victims of the oppressive regimes as it was in the officials. The people wanted to make Jesus king, not because he inaugurated among them the reign of God by preaching the good news to the poor, but because he seemed to be a better version of their earthly rulers. They wanted to replace their current institutional idols with a new idol. As Jesus says to the crowd, *You seek me, not because you saw signs* [that is, not as a locus of divine revelation], *but because you ate your fill of the loaves* [that is, because you think I could fulfill your immediate material needs better than the current regime].

Jesus refused a royalty already corrupted by the royal consciousness and functioned openly only as a prophet. As prophet he evoked the past, the covenant God made with the people in their poverty and powerlessness, and he energized them to hope for an alternative future. He announced that the reign of God would belong to the poor, the meek, the hungry, the dispossessed, the powerless. It is a reign in which mutual love among equals will replace all the hierarchical relationships built on inequality, the relationships of power and domination which structured the society of the pagans and oppressed the people of God.

But Jesus did not just promise a future reign; he acted to inaugurate it in the present. He broke the grip of the ecclesiastical establishment by declaring all religious laws except that of love

140

relative to human good and by giving free access to divine forgiveness to those who did not qualify for it by meeting institutional requirements. He broke the grip of the political establishment by declaring the equality of people as children of God called to mutual love and thus announcing the relativity of Rome's dominion in the present and the inevitability of this demise when the reign of God would come in all its fullness. He broke down the barriers of stratified society so necessary for hierarchy to function by eating with sinners, consorting with Samaritans and pagans, and calling women to be disciples and apostles along with men. Jesus the prophet reminded the people that God's covenant was still effective, announced the reign which was coming, and inaugurated it among them. But he avoided identifying himself publicly as a king until the moment when he was beyond the corrupting reach of the royal consciousness in the people, as the victim of the royal consciousness in the institution. Only when he was definitely involved in the ultimate reversal that characterizes the divine reign, in the poverty and powerlessness of death from which only God could rescue him, did he claim his royal identity. From the cross he reigned as king.

(*New Wineskins*, 278-280)

Sandra M. Schneiders, a member of the Congregation of the Sisters, Servants of the Immaculate Heart of Mary of Monroe, Michigan, since 1955, is associate professor of New Testament and Christian Spirituality, a staff member of the Institute for Spirituality and Worship at the Jesuit School of Theology, and a member of the doctoral faculty in scripture and spirituality at the Graduate Theological Union in Berkeley, California. She received the S.T.L. from the Institut Catholique in Paris and the S.T.D. from the Gregorian University in Rome.

Presentation of the Lord

Gospel: Luke 2:22-40

When the day came to purify them according to the law of Moses, the couple brought Jesus up to Jerusalem so that he could be presented to the Lord.

Commentary: John Paul II

Forty days after the nativity the Church celebrates an event full of spiritual significance. On that day the Son of God, as a tiny child of poor parents, born in a rough stable in Bethlehem, was carried to the temple in Jerusalem. This was his own temple, the temple of the living God, but he came to it not as the Lord but as one under the law. For the poor the law prescribed that forty days after the birth of the firstborn two turtle-doves or two young pigeons must be offered in sacrifice, as a sign that the child was consecrated to the Lord.

The message which the Spirit of God allowed the old man Simeon to sense and express so wonderfully was implicitly in the event itself, in this first encounter between the Messiah and his temple. On seeing the child, Simeon begins to utter words that are not of human provenance. He prophesies, prompted by the Holy Spirit; he speaks with the voice of God, the God for whom the temple was built and who is its rightful master.

Simeon's words begin, in what the liturgy calls the Song, by bearing witness to the light, and in so doing they ante-date by thirty years the witness borne by John the Baptist. They end, on the other hand, by bearing the first witness to the cross, in which contradiction of Jesus, the Christ, is to find tangible expression. The cost of the cross was shared by the mother, whose soul—according to Simeon's words—was to be pierced by a sword, *so that the thoughts of many hearts may be laid bare.*

Chronologically the presentation of Jesus in the temple is linked with the nativity, but in its significance it belongs with the mystery of the pasch. It is the first of the events which clearly reveal the messianic status of the newborn child. With him are linked the fall and the rising of many in the old Israel and also the new. On him the future of humankind depends. It is he who is the true Lord of the ages to come. His reign begins when the temple sacrifice is offered in accordance with the law, and it attains full realization through the sacrifice on the cross, offered in accordance with an eternal plan of love.

(*Sign of Contradiction,* 40-41)

John Paul II (1920-), born Karol Wojtyla, was ordained a priest in 1946, a bishop in 1958, made a cardinal in 1967, and elected pope in 1978. Hewn from the colossus of Polish Catholicism, formed by the discipline of study and manual labor, his physical, moral, and intellectual strength has been the rock on which the grace of God has built up the Church during a period of consolidation after Vatican II. His particular insights into the human condition, shaped by his interest in the theater, his gifts for poetry and play writing, and his study of personalist philosophy, have contributed much to the teaching of the Church.

Saints Peter and Paul

Gospel: Matthew 16:13-19

When Jesus had appeared to his disciples and had eaten with them, he said to Simon Peter, "Simon, son of John, do you love me more than these?" "Yes, Lord," Peter said, "you know that I love you." At which Jesus said, "Feed my lambs."

Commentary: J. Bonsirven

In Palestine, the only solid foundation people knew was rock—*Kepha* in Aramaic. Simon, son of John, was to be this foundation. By this metaphor, an exalted rank in the Church, the primacy, was assigned to Peter, and its rights and prerogatives would become apparent as they were exercised. Paul, when he speaks of Christ as the chief cornerstone in the edifice of the Church, does not hesitate to call the apostles and the prophets the foundation on which the Church is built. There are some words of his which bear witness to the fact that the early Christians called Simon *Kepha* and acknowledged that his was a position of real primacy.

This was the first time Jesus mentioned his Church. Like Christ himself and all that he was doing, the Church was to be the target for the attacks of hostile powers represented here by "the gates of Hades," Hades being thought of then as the abode of the wicked, while in poetic style the gates designated a fortress. The satanic powers would not prevail against either the society or the rock which upheld it. The reign of God continued to triumph over the devil. In fact, the phrases which follow seem to identify the Church with the reign of God; Jesus has the power of a ruler in both of them. He appointed Peter Grand Vizier, the governor of the kingdom. His extensive power is symbolized by the keys, which the master of the house withdrew and handed over to his true servant. This authority is also indicated by the power to "bind and loose," words used in the rabbinical vocabulary to designate the power of the judiciary and the legislature.

The primacy of Peter is once again implied in the promise made to him on the eve of the passion. This event is compared with the act of sifting corn; only the good grain remains in the riddle: all the rest, straw, bad grain, soil, is thrown out. In the same way, the faith of the apostles was to be violently disturbed by the great ordeal. Their leader would not be overcome completely, and once he had returned to his original loyalty, would strengthen his brethren and direct them in their faith.

Peter was confirmed in his dignity later by our Lord after his resurrection—it was after his triumph that the Church was to show signs of autonomous life. We know the dialogue which was exchanged on the banks of the Sea of Tiberias amid the splendor of the rising sun. The Master wanted to make it clear to Simon by his thrice-repeated question that his office demanded a greater degree of love: the leader, more than anyone, must share the infinite charity of the supreme head. His official title was "shepherd." God called himself the shepherd of his people and gave the same title to the prophets, and especially to the Messiah. Jesus also described himself as the "good shepherd," proving his love for his flock by the sacrifice of his life. He made Peter his colleague and deputy in this pastoral ministry, which included the care and direction of the faithful.

(*The Theology of the New Testament*, 66-69)

Joseph Bonsirven (1880-1958), after his education and ordination at the Sulpician seminary in Paris, was assigned to teach scripture at the major seminary of Albi. In 1906 he studied at the École Biblique under Père Lagrange; in 1909 he received his licentiate in sacred scripture from the Pontifical Biblical Commission. The following year his doctoral thesis on rabbinic eschatology was not accepted, and he was forbidden to teach scripture. Bonsirven humbly accepted the decision and returned to his diocese for pastoral work, which was interrupted by service and subsequent imprisonment in World War I. While a prisoner of war, he was appointed by Benedict XV to teach dogmatic theology and scripture to imprisoned seminarians. After the war he joined the Society of Jesus and returned to teaching New Testament exegesis in France and then in Rome at the Biblical Institute.

Transfiguration of the Lord

Gospel: Matthew 17:1-9

Jesus took Peter, James, and his brother John and led them up a high mountain by themselves. He was transfigured before their eyes. His face became as dazzling as the sun, his clothes as radiant as light.

Commentary: J. Corbon

What took place in this unexpected event? Why did the Incomprehensible One allow his "elusive beauty" to be glimpsed for a moment in the body of the world? Two certainties can serve us as guides. First, the change, or, to transliterate the Greek word, the "metamorphosis," was not a change in Jesus. The gospel text and the unanimous interpretation of the Fathers are clear: Christ "was transfigured, not by acquiring what he was not but by manifesting to his disciples what he in fact was; he opened their eyes and gave these blind men sight." The change is on the side of the disciples. The second certainty confirms this point: the purpose of the transfiguration, like everything else in the economy that is revealed in the Bible, is the salvation of human beings. As in the burning bush, so here the Word "allows" the light of his divinity "to be seen" in his body, in order to communicate not knowledge but life and salvation; he reveals himself by giving himself and he gives himself in order to transform us into himself.

But if it be permissible to take off the sandals of curiosity and inquisitive gnosis and draw near to the mystery, we may ask: Why did Jesus choose this particular moment, these two witnesses and these three apostles? What was he, the Son—so passionately in love with the Father and so passionately concerned for us—experiencing in his heart? A few days before Peter had already been given an interior enlightenment and had acknowledged Jesus as the Christ of God. Jesus had then begun to lift the veil from the not far distant ending of his life: he had to suffer, be put to death, and be raised from the dead. It is between this first prediction and

146

the second that he undertakes to ascend the mountain. The reason for the transfiguration can be glimpsed, therefore, in what the evangelists do not say: having finished the instruction preparatory to his own Pasch, Jesus is determined to advance to its accomplishment. With the whole of his being, the whole of his "body," he is committed to the loving will of the Father; he accepts that will without reservation. From now on, everything, up to and including the final struggle at which the same three disciples will be invited to be present, will be an expression of his unconditional "Yes" to the Father's love.

We must certainly enter into this mystery of committed love if we are to understand that the transfiguration is not an impossible unveiling of the light of the Word to the eyes of the apostles, but rather a moment of intensity in which the entire being of Jesus is utterly united with the compassion of the Father. During these decisive days of his life he becomes transparent to the light of the love of the One who gives himself to human beings for their salvation. The radiance of the light in the suffering body of Jesus is as it were the thrill experienced by the Father in response to the total self-giving of his only Son. This explains the voice that pierces through the cloud: "This is my Son, the Beloved; he enjoys my favor. Listen to him" (Mt 17:5).

(The Wellspring of Worship, 60-61)

Jean Corbon is a member of the Dominican community of Beirut and author of the book *L'Église des Arabes*. His whole thrust in writing on liturgy is to rediscover its meaning and to understand how the whole of life finds itself transformed.

Assumption of Mary

Gospel: Luke 9:39-56

Mary set out, proceeding in haste into the hill country to a town of Judah, where she entered Zechariah's house and greeted Elizabeth.

Commentary: L. Bouyer

Mary should be looked on as the living pledge of Christ's promises to the Church: that where he is, we also shall be; then the glory given him by the Father he will give to us, as he received it.

Consequently, it goes without saying that Mary's Assumption is, by no means, a kind of apotheosis dispensing her from the common human destiny, any more than the Immaculate Conception was an abnormal privilege designed to emancipate her from the conditions of human life. But, as Mary, by the grace of redemption brought by her Son, a grace to which, in opening herself, she opened the whole of humankind, was the first to be saved, and that more perfectly than any other person, as regards sin, so she is seen as saved the first and more perfectly than anyone else, as regards death, the result of sin. Her Immaculate Conception was the pledge of the perfect and wholly virginal purity to which, one day, the creature, sullied by sin, has to attain, in order to become the Spouse of Christ. Likewise, her Assumption is the pledge of the glory Christ will give to his spouse, as he has already given it to his mother. As John says: *It has not yet appeared what we shall be. We know that, when he shall appear, we shall be like to him, because we shall see him as he is.* For Mary, this condition is already realized. Her perfect faith passed, as it were, without any intermediate stage to sight. In the mother of Christ and our mother, we are given the pledge of his promise; seeing him as she sees him, we shall be like to her, who is already like to him. As Paul says: *We shall be taken up together to meet Christ, and so we shall always be with the Lord.*

How, then, are we to represent, as far as is possible, this state of glory, of eschatology already realized, to which Mary has entered in the train of her Son?

Christ's ascension does not mean that he has left us to our present condition, since he has gone only to prepare a place for us, that where he is we also may be; no more does Mary's assumption mean her separation from us. As her son is represented in the letter to the Hebrews as *always living to intercede for us*, so she remains, as the constant belief of the Church assures us, at his side, the interceder par excellence. Already her blessedness is perfect, present, as she is, with God who has placed in her his delight. But, more than ever, the contemplative prayer which raises her above the angels, in the bliss of an eternal eucharist, carries an irresistible intercession, on her part, that sinners, all of us countless children of hers, may come to be united to her in her Son.

(*The Seat of Wisdom*, 202-203)

Louis Bouyer (1913-), born of Protestant parents, became a Lutheran minister until, as he says, "his profound studies into the nature of Protestantism as a genuinely spiritual movement led him gradually to the recognition that Catholicism was the only Church in which the positive elements of the Reformation could be exercised." He became a priest of the French Oratory and professor of spiritual theology at the *Institut Catholique* in Paris. He has written extensively on both ecumenism and liturgy.

Triumph of the Holy Cross

Gospel: John 3:13-17

No one has gone up to heaven except the one who came down from there—the Son of Man. Just as Moses lifted up the serpent in the desert, so must the Son of Man be lifted up, that all who believe may have eternal life in him.

Commentary: A. Bloom

The Lord himself has taken upon his shoulder the first cross, the heaviest, most appalling cross, but after him thousands and thousands of men, women, and children have taken upon themselves their own crosses, lesser crosses, but how often these crosses, which are lesser than Christ's, remain so frightening for us. Innumerable crowds of people have lovingly, obediently, walked in the footsteps of Christ, treading the long tragic way which is shown by our Lord, a way tragic but which leads from this earth to the very throne of God, into the kingdom of God. They walk, carrying their crosses, they walk now for two thousand years, those who believe in Christ. They walk on, following him, crowd after crowd, and on the way we see crosses, innumerable crosses, on which are crucified the disciples of Christ.

Crosses, one cross after the other, and however far we look, it is crosses and crosses again. We see the bodies of the martyrs, we see the heroes of the spirit, we see monks and nuns, we see priests and pastors, but many, many more people do we see, ordinary, simple, humble people of God who have willingly taken upon themselves the cross of Christ. There is no end to this procession. They walk throughout the centuries knowing that Christ has foretold us that they will have sorrow on this earth, but that the kingdom of God is theirs.

They walk with the heavy cross, rejected, hated, because of truth, because of the name of Christ. They walk, they walk, these pure victims of God, the old and young, children and grown-ups.

But where are we? Are we going to stand and look; to see this long procession, this throng of people with shining eyes, with hope unquenched, with unfaltering love, with incredible joy in their hearts, pass us by? Shall we not join them, this eternally moving crowd, that is marked as a crowd of victims, but also as little children of the kingdom? Are we not going to take up our cross and follow Christ? Christ has commanded us to follow him. He has invited us to the banquet of his kingdom, and he is at the head of the procession. Nay, he is together with each of those who walk. Is this a nightmare? How can blood and flesh endure this tragedy, the sight of all these martyrs, new and old? Because Christ is risen, because we do not see in the Lord who walks ahead of us the defeated prophet of Galilee as he was seen by his tormentors, his persecutors. We know him now in the glory of the resurrection. We know that every word of his is true. We know that the kingdom of God is ours if we simply follow him.

(*Meditations—A Spiritual Journey*, 123-125)

Anthony Bloom (1914-), Metropolitan of Sourozh, born Andre Borisovich Bloom in Lausanne, Switzerland, was educated at the Sorbonne, became a doctor of medicine before taking monastic vows in 1943 and became a priest of the Russian Orthodox Church in Paris in 1948. In 1960 he was ordained archbishop of Sourozh and then became in 1965 Metropolitan and Patriarch of Moscow and All Russia in Western Europe. He lectured in various parts of the world and authored many books on prayer and the spiritual life.

All Saints

Gospel: Matthew 5:1-12

When Jesus saw the crowds he went up on the mountainside. After he had sat down his disciples gathered around him, and he began to teach them: "Blessed are the poor in spirit; the reign of God is theirs."

Commentary: K. Adam

Hosts of the redeemed are continually passing into heaven, either directly or by the road of purification in the suffering Church. They pass into the presence of the Lamb and of him who sits upon the throne, in order face to face—and no longer in mere similitude and image—to contemplate the Trinity, in whose bosom are all possibilities and all realities, the unborn God from out of whose eternal well-spring of life all beings drink existence and strength, motion and beauty, truth and love. There is none there who has not been brought home by God's mercy alone. All are redeemed, from the highest seraph to the new-born child just sealed by the grace of baptism as it left the world. Delivered from all selfish limitations and raised above all earthly anxieties, they live, within that sphere of love which their life on earth has traced out for them, the great life of God. It is true life, no idle stagnation, but a continual activity of sense and mind and will. It is true that they can merit no longer, nor bear fruit now for the kingdom of heaven. For the kingdom of heaven is established and grace has finished its work. But the life of glory is far richer than the life of grace. The infinite spaces of the being of God, in all its width and depth, provide a source in which the soul seeks and finds the satisfaction of its most intimate yearnings. New possibilities continually reveal themselves, new vistas of truth, new springs of joy. Being incorporated in the most sacred humanity of Jesus, the soul is joined in most mysterious intimacy to the Godhead itself. It hears the heartbeats of God and feels the deep life that pulsates within the Divinity. The soul is set and lives at the center of all being, whence the sources of all life flow, where the meaning of all existence shines forth in the triune God, where all power and all beauty, all peace and all blessedness, are become pure actuality and purest present, are made an eternal now.

This life of the saints, in its superabundant and inexhaustible fruitfulness, is at the same time a life of the richest variety and fullness. The one Spirit of Jesus, their head and mediator, is manifested in his saints in all the rich variety of their individual lives, and according to the various measures in which every single soul, with its own special gifts and its own special call, has received and employed the grace of God. The one conception of the saint, of the servant of Christ, is embodied in an infinite variety of forms. The litany of the saints takes us rapidly through this "celestial hierarchy." And while every name denotes a special gift, a special character, a special life, yet all are united in one only love and in one gospel of joy and gladness.

(*The Spirit of Catholicism,* 120-122)

Karl Adam (1876-1966) was born in Bavaria, studied for the priesthood and was ordained in 1900. After some experience of pastoral work he taught first at the University of Munich and in 1918 became a professor at Strasbourg. A year later he was appointed to the chair of dogmatic theology at Tübingen, which he held until 1949. He was among the forerunners of ecumenism, liberal and up to date in thought, but always orthodox. His writings, which had great influence especially on the laity, include: *The Nature of Catholicism, Christ Our Brother,* and *The Son of God.*

All Souls

Gospel: Luke 7:11-17

Jesus went to a town called Naim, accompanied by his disciples and a great number of people. When he was near the gate of the town, it happened that a dead man was being carried out for burial, the only son of his mother, and she was a widow.

Commentary: Catherine of Genoa

There is no joy save that in paradise
to be compared with the joy of the souls in purgatory.
As the rust of sin is consumed
the soul is more and more open to God's love.
Just as a covered object left out in the sun
cannot be penetrated by the sun's rays,
in the same way,
once the covering of the soul is removed,
the soul opens itself fully to the rays of the sun.
Having become one with God's will,
these souls, to the extent that he grants it to them,
see into God.
Joy in God, oneness with him, is the end of these souls,
an instinct implanted in them at their creation.
All that I have said
is as nothing compared to what I feel within,
the witnessed correspondence of love
between God and the soul;
for when God sees the soul pure as it was in its origins,
he tugs at it with a glance,
draws it and binds it to himself with a fiery love.
God so transforms the soul in himself
that it knows nothing other than God.
He will not cease
until he has brought the soul to its perfection.
That is why the soul seeks to cast off

any and all impediments, so that it can be lifted up to God;
and such impediments
are the cause of the suffering of the souls in purgatory.
Not that the souls dwell on their suffering;
they dwell rather on the resistance they feel in themselves
against the will of God,
against his intense and pure love bent on nothing
but draw them up to him.
And I see rays of lightning
darting from that divine love to the creature,
so intense and fiery as to annihilate not the body alone
but, were it possible, the soul.
The soul becomes like gold
that becomes purer as it is fired,
all dross being cast out.
The last stage of love
is that which does its work without human doing.
If humans were to be aware
of the many hidden flaws in them
they would despair.
These flaws are burned away in the last stage of love.
God then shows the soul its weakness,
so that the soul may see the workings of God.
If we are to become perfect,
change must be brought about in us and without us;
that is, the change is to be the work not of human beings but of God.
This, the last stage of love,
is the pure and intense love of God alone.
The overwhelming love of God
gives the soul a joy beyond words.
In purgatory great joy and great suffering
do not exclude one another.

(Purgation and Purgatory, 71-82)

Catherine of Genoa (1447-1510) was married at the age of sixteen to Giuliano Adorno. After ten unhappy years she was suddenly converted to ardent love of God. Later her husband too was converted and helped her to care for the sick in a hospital at Genoa. Her teachings, compiled by others, are contained in *Purgation and Purgatory* and *The Spiritual Dialogue*.

Dedication
of the Lateran Basilica

Gospel: Luke 19:1-10

Entering Jericho, Jesus passed through the city. There was a man there named Zacchaeus, the chief tax collector and a wealthy man. He was trying to see what Jesus was like, but being small of stature, was unable to do so because of the crowd.

Commentary: H. de Lubac

The mystery of the Church is our own mystery par excellence, for it is in his Church that God looks upon us and loves us, in her that he desires us and we encounter him, and in her that we cleave to him and are made blessed. She is the mountain visible from afar, the radiant city, the light set on a candlestick to illuminate the whole house. She is the "continual miracle" which is always announcing to people the coming of their Savior and manifesting his liberating power in examples without number; she is the magnificent vaulting under which the saints, like so many stars, sing together of the glory of the redeemer.

To a person who lives in her mystery she is always the city of precious stones, the heavenly Jerusalem, the bride of the Lamb, as she was to Saint John; and seeing her thus, he feels that very joy which bursts through the light-split skies of the Apocalypse and glows in its serene visions. One begins to understand what made Saint Augustine cry: "When I talk about her, I cannot stop."

Saint Clement of Alexandria said superbly, "Just as the will of God is an act, and is called the world, so also his intention is the salvation of all people, and is called the Church." So we should say of the Church, as of Christ, that her kingdom *shall be without end*, for the *nuptials of the Lamb* are eternal. For the elect salvation consists in being welcomed into the heart of the Church for which they were created, in which they have been predestined and are loved.

Holy Church has two lives, one in time and the other in eternity. We must always keep a firm hold on the continuity of the one Church through the diversity of her successive states. Prior to the incarnation, before she had become the bride, she was the betrothed only; and that remains true to a certain extent until the end of time, in that the mystical marriage of Nazareth and Calvary needs the final parousia as its fulfillment. All the same, the Church has already received an incomparable betrothal gift, since her bridegroom has given her his very blood.

It is one and the same Church that is to see God face to face, bathed in his glory, and yet is our actual Church, progressing laboriously in our world, militant and on pilgrimage, humiliated daily in a hundred ways. In the depths of her being she is already the city of God; through the virtue of faith she has already been brought into the storerooms of the king. This holy Jerusalem is, mysteriously and in hope, the heavenly Jerusalem; our earthly mother is already our heavenly mother, and the doors which she opens to us are already the heavenly gates. There will be yet one more changing of brass into gold and iron into silver; but in and through this future transmutation she will always be "the same city of Yahweh, the Zion of holy Israel": "This is heavenly and that is heavenly; this is Jerusalem and that is Jerusalem." We ought, indeed, to love that very element in the Church which is transitory, but we ought to love it as the one and only means, the indispensable organ, the providential instrument; and at the same time as the pledge, the passing image, the promise of the communion to come.

(*The Splendor of the Church,* 25-54, passim)

Henri de Lubac (1886-1991), after the study of law, entered the Society of Jesus in 1913 at Saint Leonary in Great Britain and taught fundamental theology at the Catholic Faculty of Lyon. With Cardinal Daniélou he founded in 1940 the series *Sources Chrétiennes.* From 1960 onward he was a member of various Vatican commissions in preparation for the Council, and after the Council continued to work on various commissions. He was created a cardinal by Pope John Paul II in 1983. He authored numerous books and articles, his book *Catholicism* being his masterpiece. Cardinal de Lubac died in 1991.

Immaculate Conception

Gospel: Luke 1:26-38

The angel Gabriel was sent from God to a town of Galilee named Nazareth, to a virgin betrothed to a man named Joseph, of the house of David. The virgin's name was Mary. Upon arriving, the angel said to her: "Rejoice, O highly favored daughter, the Lord is with you. Blessed are you among women."

Commentary: R. Knox

The feast of our Lady's Immaculate Conception, which we celebrate today, is the promise and the earnest of Christmas; our salvation is already in the bud. As the first green shoot heralds the approach of spring, in a world that is frost-bound and seems dead, so in a world of great sinfulness and of utter despair that spotless conception heralds the restoration of man's innocence. As the shoot gives unfailing promise of the flower which is to spring from it, this conception gives unfailing promise of the virgin birth. Life had come into the world again, supernatural life, not of man's choosing or of man's fashioning. And it grew there unmarked by human eyes; no angels sang over the hills to celebrate it, no shepherds left their flocks to come and see; no wise men were beckoned by the stars to witness that prodigy. And yet the first Advent had begun. Our Lady, you see, is the consummation of the Old Testament; with her, the cycle of history begins anew. When God created the first Adam, he made his preparations beforehand; he fashioned a paradise ready for him to dwell in. And when he restored our nature in the second Adam, once more there was a preparation to be made beforehand. He fashioned a paradise for the second Adam to dwell in, and that paradise was the body and soul of our blessed Lady, immune from the taint of sin, Adam's curse. It was winter still in all the world around; but in the quiet home where Saint Anne gave birth to her daughter, spring had begun.

Man's winter, God's spring; the living branch growing from the dead root; for that, year by year, we Christians give thanks to God when Advent comes round. It is something that has happened once for all; we look for no further redemption, no fresh revelation, however many centuries are to roll over this earth before the skies crack above us and our Lord comes in judgment. Yet there are times in history when the same mood comes upon us, even upon us Christians; the same mood of despair in which the world, Jewish and heathen, was sunk at the time when Jesus Christ was born. There are times when the old landmarks seem obliterated, and the old certainties by which we live have deserted us; the world seems to have exhausted itself, and has no vigor left to face its future; the only forces which seem to possess any energy are those which make for disruption and decay. The world's winter, and it is always followed by God's spring.

Behold, I make all things new, said our Lord to the saint of the Apocalypse; let us rejoice, on this feast of the Immaculate Conception, in the proof and pledge he has given us of that inexhaustible fecundity which belongs only to his grace. And let us ask our blessed Lady to win for us, in our own lives, that continual renewal of strength and holiness which befits our supernatural destiny. Fresh graces, not soiled by the memory of past failure; fresh enterprise, to meet the conditions of a changing world; fresh hope, to carry our burdens beyond the shifting scene of this present world into the changeless repose of eternity.

(*University and Plain Sermons,* 402-405)

Ronald Knox (1881-1951), son of E. A. Knox, one-time bishop of Manchester, England, was educated at Eton and Oxford. Already noted for the brilliance of his mind, he was appointed chaplain of Trinity College, Oxford, and became a leading figure among Anglo-Catholics. In 1917 he was received into the Roman Catholic Church and ordained two years later. He taught for a time at Saint Edmund's Ware and was chaplain to the Catholic undergraduates at Oxford from 1936 to 1939. At the request of the hierarchy he then devoted himself to making a new English translation of the entire bible. The New Testament was first published in 1945 and the Old in 1949. As a writer on a wide range of subjects, Knox's thought is often strikingly original and his style characterized by wit.

Acknowledgments

In an anthology of readings it is sometimes difficult to locate all the copyright holders of the individual readings selected. Over the years the copyright holder may have transferred the rights to another company, or the copyright has reverted to another entity. Also there are changes of address, for several requests have been returned.

If I have failed to acknowledge a copyright, please bring it to my attention, and a correction will take place.

When copyright has expired or when a text is translated from the original language, no copyright is mentioned. Thank you.

Anthony Bloom, *Beginning to Pray* (Denville: Dimension Books, 1971).

Pierre Bernard, O.P., *The Mystery of Jesus*, ©1966 Alba House.

Joseph Bonsirven, S.J., *The Theology of the New Testament* (Wellwood, England: Search Press, Ltd-Burns and Oates, Ltd.).

Ladislaus Boros, *God Is With Us*, ©1967 Burns and Oates, Ltd.

Catherine of Genoa, *Purgation and Purgatory, The Spiritual Dialogue*, translated by Serge Hughes, ©1979 by the Missionary Society of Saint Paul the Apostle in the State of New York. Used by permission of Paulist Press.

Catherine of Siena, *The Dialogue*, translated by Suzanne Noffke, O.P., © 1980 by the Missionary Society of Saint Paul the Apostle in the State of New York. Used by permission of Paulist Press.

Teilhard de Chardin, *Le Milieu Divin*, ©1960 Harper and Rowe.

Jean Corbon, *The Wellspring of Worship*, translated by Matthew O'Connell. English translation ©1988 by the Missionary Society of Saint Paul the Apostle in the State of New York. Used by permission of Paulist Press.

Jean Daniélou, S.J., *Le mystère de l'Avent*, ©Editions du Seuil (reprinted by permission of Georges Borchardt, Inc.).

Demetrius Dumm, *Flowers in the Desert, A Spirituality of the Bible*, ©1987 Paulist Press. Used by permission of Paulist Press.

Elizabeth of the Trinity, *I Have Found God*, The Complete Works, Volume I, © 1984 Washington Province of Discalced Carmelites, Inc.

Hildegard of Bingen, *Scivias*, translated by Mother Columba Hart and Jane Bishop, ©1990 Abbey of Regina Laudis: Benedictine Congregation Regina Laudis of the Strict Observance, inc. Used by permission of Paulist Press.

Frances Caryll Houselander, *The Reed of God*, ©1954 Sheed and Ward (London).

Anthony di Mello, *The Way to Love,* © 1991 Gujarat Dahitya Prakash. Used by permission of Doubleday.

Geoffrey Preston, O.P., *God's Way to Be Human, Meditations on Following Christ,* ©1978 English Province of the Order of Preachers. Used by permission of Paulist Press.

Karl Rahner, *Biblical Homilies,* translated by Desmond Forristal and Richard Strachan, ©1966 Sheed and Ward (London).

Rudolph Schnackenburg, *New Testament for Spiritual Reading,* ©1963 Herder and Herder.

Sandra Schneiders, *New Wineskins,* © 1986 by the Missionary Society of Saint Paul the Apostle in the State of New York. Used by permission of Paulist Press.

Max Thurian, *Mary, Mother of All Christians,* © 1964. Herder and Herder, New York.

Jean Vanier, *Jesus the Gift of Love,* © 1994. Used by permission of the Crossroad Publishing Company (New York).

Jean Vanier, *Be Not Afraid,* © 1975. Used by permission of Paulist Press.

Index of Scripture

Index of Authors

Also available from New City Press in the same series:

Meditations on the Sunday Gospels

JOHN ROTELLE, O.S.A.(ed.)

"*Meditations on the Sunday Gospels, Year A,* is a fine resourse for both preachers and 'ponderers' of the Sunday readings."

Kathleen Hughes, R.S.C.J.
Catholic Theological Union, Chicago, Illinois

"John Rotelle is to be congratulated warmly on this first volume in what will, in time, be an indispensable series on the three-year cycle of the Sunday Gospel."

Dr. Michael Jackson
Christ Anglican Church, Oxford, England

Year A
ISBN 1-56548-032-5
paper, 5 3/8 x 8 1/2, 168 pp., $9.95

Year B
ISBN 1-56548-082-1
paper, 5 3/8 x 8 1/2, 168 pp., $9.95

To order call 1 (800) 462-5980

Journey with the Fathers
Commentaries on the Sunday Gospels

EDITH BARNECUT, O.S.B. (ed.)
Foreword by JOHN E. ROTELLE, O.S.A.

"Each Sunday Gospel is adorned with a reading from one of the early classic writers. The selection is appropriate not only for preparing homilies but also for prayerful meditation."

The Bible Today

"Special care has been taken in making the translations so they may be proclaimed effectively. There is a brief introduction to the life and ministry of each author included in the collection."

Worship

Year A
ISBN 1-56548-013-9, **2d printing**
paper, 5 3/8 x 8 1/2, 168 pp., $9.95

Year B
ISBN 1-56548-056-2, **2d printing**
paper, 5 3/8 x 8 1/2, 160 pp., $9.95

Year C
ISBN 1-56548-064-3, **2d printing**
paper, 5 3/8 x 8 1/2, 160 pp., $9.95

To order call 1 (800) 462-5980